BELIEVING
Jesus

BELIEVING JESUS

Are You Willing to Risk Everything?

A Journey Through the Book of ACTS

Lisa Harper

W PUBLISHING GROUP

AN IMPRINT OF THOMAS NELSON

Published in Nashville, Tennessee, by W Publishing Group, an imprint of Thomas Nelson. Thomas Nelson is a registered trademark of HarperCollins Christian Publishing, Inc.

Thomas Nelson titles may be purchased in bulk for educational, business, fund-raising, or sales promotional use. For information, please e-mail SpecialMarkets@ThomasNelson.com.

Any Internet addresses, phone numbers, or company or product information printed in this book are offered as a resource and are not intended in any way to be or to imply an endorsement by Thomas Nelson, nor does Thomas Nelson vouch for the existence, content, or services of these sites, phone numbers, companies, or products beyond the life of this book.

Scripture quotations marked NCV are taken from the New Century Version®. © 2005 by Thomas Nelson, Inc. Used by permission. All rights reserved.

Scripture quotations marked ESV are taken from THE ENGLISH STANDARD VERSION. © 2001 by Crossway Bibles, a division of Good News Publishers. Used by permission. All rights reserved.

Scripture quotations marked MSG are taken from *The Message* by Eugene H. Peterson. © 1993, 1994, 1995, 1996, 2000. Used by permission of NavPress Publishing Group. All rights reserved.

Scripture quotations marked NIV are taken from the HOLY BIBLE: NEW INTERNATIONAL VERSION®, NIV®. © 1973, 1978, 1984, 2011 by Biblica, Inc.™ Used by permission of Zondervan. All rights reserved worldwide. www.zondervan.com.

Scripture quotations marked NLT are taken from the Holy Bible, New Living Translation, © 1996, 2004, 2007 by Tyndale House Foundation. Used by permission of Tyndale House Publishers, Inc., Carol Stream, IL 60188. All rights reserved.

Scripture quotations marked KJV are taken from the King James Version of the Bible.

Scripture quotations marked THE VOICE are taken from The Voice™. © 2012 by Ecclesia Bible Society. Used by permission. All rights reserved. Note: Italics in quotations from The Voice are used to "indicate words not directly tied to the dynamic translation of the original language" but that "bring out the nuance of the original, assist in completing ideas, and . . . provide readers with information that would have been obvious to the original audience" (The Voice, preface).

Library of Congress Cataloging-in-Publication Data Is Available Upon Request

ISBN 978-0-8499-2197-1

Printed in the United States of America

15 16 17 18 19 RRD 6 5 4 3 2 1

To my brave and beautiful daughter, Melissa Price Harper. You are a tangible reminder of God's kindness, and I love you with all my heart.

I've pitched my tent in the land of hope.
—ACTS 2:26 THE MESSAGE

Contents

ONE

The Cost of Discipleship

Fear and disillusionment. Courage and commitment. Intense emotion and unbridled passion. The ultimate risk of life in exchange for undeserved grace and a treasured spot in eternity. An example for billions of people who would follow the same road centuries and millennia later. An all-out quest by a growing number of believers to risk everything to spread Jesus Christ's message around the world. The book of Acts. Wow.

Have you ever fully dug into this amazing book? I mean really dug in, where your heart beats faster with each revelation and you can't wait to turn the page to see what happens next? All the time you're imagining what it would've been like to have been there beside them. That's what we're going to do in this book, and I cannot wait to take the journey with you.

But first, I need to tell you a story about a precious child who is very close to my heart. In fact, the only person closer to my heart is Jesus, and that's where it all connects. . . .

Mama blanc. White mama. That's what my little girl, Missy, called me the first time we met in Haiti in June 2012. And she didn't say it while batting her eyelashes and wearing a sweet smile. Nope. She was pretty much scowling with suspicion. She was two and a half years old and about nineteen pounds soaking wet, but man was she feisty. When her caregiver went to place her in my arms, I think what she *wanted* to say was, "Don't even think about holding me, you giant pale chick!" but she only spoke a few words of English at the time. Even speaking Creole was difficult because her little lungs were filled with fluid and weakened with tuberculosis. I was holding a bowl of rice and beans, though, which surely made her stomach growl. So instead of dissing me on the spot, she eyed me with a mixture of wariness and hunger. Then she did something remarkable; she reached out and wrapped her fist around my little finger with surprising strength and rasped, "Halo, mama blanc."

On that sweltering June day in 2012, about fifty kilometers southwest of Port-au-Prince, I became a tangible reality to my daughter. She saw and heard and touched me for the first time. She sure as heck didn't trust me at that point though. I was just a large, sweaty, non-Haitian woman. Several visits and suitcases bursting with presents later, Missy had warmed up to me considerably. I'd basically become Santa with bigger hips. The adoption process included two long years and five trips to the hottest place on the planet; in fact, there were times I promised Jesus I'd be a missionary in Africa if He'd just make a Slurpee materialize in front of me. But by the end of it, Missy liked me a lot. I'd become something akin to Barney, only without the obnoxious vocal inflection and purple hue.

But it wasn't until after Missy had come home to live with me in Tennessee—*after* we'd twirled and wiggled through hours of charades in our quest to communicate (her English was very limited when the adoption was finalized, and my Creole is abysmal); *after* I'd rocked her through many nights when she couldn't sleep; *after* I'd held her during way too many blood draws at Vanderbilt Children's Hospital (Missy's birth mom died of AIDS and unwittingly infected her with HIV); *after* I'd slipped not once, not twice, but *three* times in wee ponds she'd created by cramming copious wads of toilet paper in a commode and then flushing it over and over again with unrestrained glee (toilets were a luxury in her village, even more so toilet paper, so she was initially quite enamored with it); *after* we'd discovered a shared affinity for Pirate's Booty (the best popcorn *ever*), belly laughs, loud worship tunes (especially those with a very active drum track), enthusiastic dancing, roller coasters, pistachios, and playing tag on the beach; and only *after* I wiped her bottom and nose and tears more times than I can count—that my baby really began to trust me.

Three weeks ago, I'd spent several minutes at bedtime explaining to Missy who'd be picking her up from school the next day. She'd be spending the weekend with her Aunt Sharon because I would be leaving on an airplane for Kansas City for work the next morning. She turned toward me and slid her chilly, five-year-old feet under the covers and stuck all ten of her perfect brown toes in my "belly fold." I've gained weight since becoming a mom, partly because I've developed a bad habit of eating some of her favorite foods—macaroni and cheese and quesadillas are at the top of her list—and partly because as a single mom I don't have the time to run like I used to and burn off the extra calories. She wiggled her toes in my newly grown valley for a minute, pondering the fact that I was going away for a few days, and then posed a poignant question. "Mama love Missy?"

I replied, "Oh yes, baby. I love you very, very, very much!" She dissolved into giggles and reframed the question into a boisterous declaration, "Mama love Missy! Mama love Missy! Mama love Missy!"

Then her eyelids got heavy, and within ninety seconds she was fast asleep with a smile on her face.

A SCENIC POINT ON THE ACTS JOURNEY

As innocent as it may seem, the ongoing transition that's taking place in Missy's and my relationship is not unlike what we're going to see played out in the book of Acts. Think about this: The disciples had spent three years with Jesus. They'd followed Him all over Galilee and traipsed behind Him to the big city of Jerusalem. Most of them had given up a lot to follow Jesus on this risky, itinerant mission, so they obviously believed *in* Him. But then things started getting dicey. Quickly. There was a riot and Jesus got carted off by the religious police. After which Pete, their unofficial team captain, panicked and threw Jesus under the bus. Then Jesus went and got Himself murdered—hung on a tree like a rabid dog between two gang-bangers. What would you think in that situation? You might still believe *in* Him, but would you fully believe what He had told you about all this?

Even though Jesus told His closest friends and followers that all this had to happen to fulfill the Old Testament prophecies, it still threw them for a loop when it did. Why? They probably thought He was being metaphorical, speaking at least a little bit figuratively. They didn't imagine their Savior would really have to die, for goodness' sake! So there, for just a moment, stretched thin as a spider's strand in redemptive history, it looked as if that small band of eleven brothers was on the verge of breaking up.

But just when it seems like this true story is going to have a tragic conclusion, the plot shifts:

> In the first book, O Theophilus, I have dealt with all that Jesus began to do and teach, until the day when he was taken up, after he had given commands through the Holy Spirit to the apostles whom he had chosen. He presented himself alive to them after his suffering by many proofs, appearing to them during forty days and speaking about the kingdom of God.
>
> And while staying with them he ordered them not to depart from Jerusalem, but to wait for the promise of

the Father, which, he said, "you heard from me; for John baptized with water, but you will be baptized with the Holy Spirit not many days from now."

So when they had come together, they asked him, "Lord, will you at this time restore the kingdom to Israel?" He said to them, "It is not for you to know times or seasons that the Father has fixed by his own authority. But you will receive power when the Holy Spirit has come upon you, and you will be my witnesses in Jerusalem and in all Judea and Samaria, and to the end of the earth." And when he had said these things, as they were looking on, he was lifted up, and a cloud took him out of their sight. And while they were gazing into heaven as he went, behold, two men stood by them in white robes, and said, "Men of Galilee, why do you stand looking into heaven? This Jesus, who was taken up from you into heaven, will come in the same way as you saw him go into heaven." (Acts 1:1–11 ESV)

Did you know that in the forty days that followed the stone being rolled away from Jesus' tomb, He appeared to more than one hundred people on at least ten separate occasions? And as for the disciples, the undeniable proof of their Redeemer's resurrection transformed them from being men who simply believed *in* Jesus to men who *believed Jesus* and all He had taught them. From watching and nodding as He preached, to preaching the same you-must-repent-and-be-born-again message themselves. From walking alongside Him to being willing to die rather than renounce their love for Him. As a matter of fact, history suggests that all of them except John ultimately died as martyrs as a direct result of their galvanized faith. They epitomized what John wrote in the twilight of his life:

> *And our brothers and sisters defeated him*
> *by the blood of the Lamb's death*
> *and by the message they preached.*
> *They did not love their lives so much*
> *that they were afraid of death.*
>
> (Revelation 12:11 NCV)

A man who was merely a man and said the sort of things Jesus said would not be a great moral teacher. He would either be a lunatic—on a level with the man who says he is a poached egg—or else he would be the Devil of Hell. You must make your choice. Either this man was, and is, the Son of God: or else a madman or something worse. You can shut Him up for a fool, you can spit at Him and kill Him as a demon; or you can fall at His feet and call Him Lord and God. But let us not come with any patronising nonsense about His being a great human teacher. He has not left that open to us. He did not intend to.

—C. S. Lewis, *Mere Christianity*[1]

ARE YOU WILLING TO RISK ACTUALLY BELIEVING JESUS?

Take a look at the declarative promises Jesus makes to His followers before He ascends into heaven to sit at the right hand of God the Father:

> But *you will* receive power when the Holy Spirit has come upon you, and *you will* be my witnesses in Jerusalem and in all Judea and Samaria, and to the end of the earth. (Acts 1:8 ESV, emphasis mine)

The original, etymological meaning of *you will* is "to grasp" or "to seize." The initiative rests with the giver.[2] In other words, these aren't gifts Christ-followers have the option of refusing. If you have put your hope in the sacrificial death and supernatural resurrection of Jesus Christ, you *will* receive power. The Greek word Luke uses here that is translated "power" in English is *dynamis,* which is also where we get the word "dynamite." This power comes from the Holy Spirit, and *youwill* be a witness to His grace and mercy. Of course, the boldness in which Christians utilize our God-given authority and communicate our faith with others will increase as we mature in our faith, but the gifts themselves are non-negotiable and non-refundable. Like an all-you-can-eat dessert bar at a weight-loss convention, these gifts show up in unlikely but oh-so-beautiful places.

Have you ever heard of Florrie Evans? By all accounts,

she was a quiet, unassuming young woman from the village of New Quay Cardiganshire, Wales. The word *cardigan* comes from a fellow who grew up in this town too—Lord Cardiganshire. Evidently, he was a tad claustrophobic, and when he once felt trapped in his long-sleeve wool military sweater, he sliced it from top to bottom in the front, thereby creating the first open-front sweater, which was named after him. But I digress. One Sunday in January 1904, Florrie felt compelled to stand up in the middle of the formal service at the Anglican sanctuary in downtown Sweater-ville and bellow with heightened emotion, "I love the Lord Jesus with all my heart!"

As amazing as it might sound, historians point to that one passionate proclamation—the powerful witness of an improbable disciple—as the starter's pistol that set the Welsh Revival of 1904–05 in motion. It was a sweeping, infectious spiritual renewal in which more than 150,000 people put their hope in Jesus, and the attention of an entire nation was turned toward God!

You see, there's an important and radical difference between the cognitive belief that Jesus is the Son of God and that He *exists* and actually *believing* Him. Believing Jesus means you're willing to risk everything you are and everything you have based on everything He taught and everything He did. It means learning to love Him more than you love your own life. It means He is your North and South. He is the Wind beneath your wings. It means nothing and nobody—and I mean *no* thing and *no* one—is more important to you than the only One who loves us unconditionally. Introverts like Florrie Evans can spark national revivals when they *believe* Jesus. Traitors like Peter can turn the tables on their own Benedict Arnold behavior and become church-building saints when they *believe* Jesus. And middle-aged, single chicks with dusty ovaries like me can become mamas when they *believe* Jesus.

WHEN PUSH COMES TO SHOVE AND RISK BECOMES REALITY

One of my oldest and dearest friends, Judy Flaherty, and I were reminiscing recently about some of our favorite memories together. We couldn't help laughing at our "blooper reel" of good times. Like the last girls' trip we took before she got married. For some crazy, probably caffeine-induced reason, we thought it'd be a great idea to drive seventeen hours one way to Yellowstone National Park. We ended up almost shivering to death in a leaky tent surrounded by big grumpy buffalo while it hailed for two days. Or the time when I crashed my mountain bike and bent the frame (and ruptured a disc in the process) at the top of a sandstone cliff in Moab, Utah, which caused us to be stranded in the desert for a few hours.

After a while it dawned on us that the memories that were the most meaningful were when we left the most proverbial skin on the pavement. They were recorded in our hearts and minds as precious because we paid such a high price for them, and unladylike scars were our currency!

I think the same could be said about life in general: the higher the cost to obtain it, the more valuable we believe it to be. That's the thematic river that's running through the book of Acts—the inestimable treasure of Jesus Christ and the exorbitant price His ancient followers were willing to pay because of their relationship with Him. Complacent Christianity simply wouldn't cut it for Luke's friends once they encountered their resurrected Savior. Oh that the same will be said of you and me one day.

> *What will people think when they hear that I'm a*
> *Jesus Freak?*
> *What will people do when they find that it's true?*
> *I don't really care if they label me a Jesus Freak*
> *Cause there ain't no disguising the truth.*[3]

Thank you, thank you, thank you to all of you who prayed for Missy and me as I brought her home from Haiti today! It's been a long, mostly wonderful journey and we are finally home safe and sound. I am grateful beyond words. #onlyGod

(Instagram post from April 14, 2014)

TWO

Earth, Wind, and Celestial Fire

When I was three or four years old, I developed a deep and abiding relationship with a lovely elderly couple. I could always count on Purda and Jim to be there when I needed them, probably because they lived purely in my imagination so they were able to sync their schedules with mine. (I'm pretty sure I fashioned these make-believe pals after a sweet couple from our church named Shirley and Darryl, who in a delightful twist of fate went on to become my youngest aunt Darlene's in-laws.) While the fictitious Purda was pudgy and loved to bake chocolate cupcakes, she wasn't above shimmying up a tree with me. Jim was a steadfast, non-yeller who spent his free time in the garage fixing things.

My mom was naturally a bit concerned about my penchant for inventing adult playmates. Family lore details her many attempts to dissuade me from hanging with Purda and Jim, but I was stubbornly committed to the relationship. Poor mom probably thought she was raising a nut-job until Grandmom brought over an article from some women's magazine claiming that children with imaginary friends have above-average intelligence. Once mom realized Purda and Jim might be harbingers of academic excellence and a Mensa membership, she breathed a sigh of relief and quit trying to talk me into betraying them.

I don't remember exactly when I stopped frolicking with those reliable yet invisible playmates; it was probably when I started kindergarten and became briefly obsessed with mastering the unicycle so I could join the circus. Much like sippy cups and hair fountains on the top of my head, they simply faded into the fabric of early childhood. But I still think about them from time to time with fondness. Although I never actually laid eyes on Jim and his spouse, I believed with all my heart they were in my corner. That they were *for me.*

Frankly, I think it would behoove us to think of the Holy Spirit in similar terms. Not the innocuous playmate part but the being perfectly for us part. I know it sounds more academic and sophisticated to say something like: the Holy Spirit is the active presence of God manifest in the tangible world. Or, the Holy Spirit is a divine component of the Trinitarian God—ontologically equal to God the Father and God the Son, who empowers, purifies, teaches, comforts, convicts, and guides those who put their faith in Jesus Christ. Either of those statements would meet most doctrinal standards, especially if intoned with a James Earl Jones kind of solemnity. Alleging that the Holy Spirit is some kind of invisible advocate just doesn't have the same doctrinal ring. Furthermore, I think many believers consider it easier—and certainly less risky—to just try to keep the Spirit of the Living God wrapped up tightly in theological jargon instead of actually grappling with who He is and how He manifests. Because like a muddy dog on white carpeting, the Holy Spirit will definitely make marks on our lives if we welcome Him in!

Speaking of messy, do you remember the sibling scandal that torpedoed Jimmy Carter's chance for reelection in 1980 when he ran against Ronald Reagan? At the beginning of President Carter's term, his younger brother Billy created the brand Billy Beer to cash in on his big brother's success. Billy seemed to delight in being depicted as a beer drinking redneck with zero political correctness. Then, as Jimmy ran against Ronald Regan, it became public that Billy had taken a $220,000 "loan" from the Libyan government to act as a liaison for oil sales. It's no wonder Carter's chief of staff Hamilton Jordan said, "This damn Billy Carter stuff is killing us!"

Even though history proved Billy Carter to be more businessman than buffoon, pretty much everybody in the Democratic Party in the late 1970s just wanted him to be quarantined and muzzled in his hometown of Plains, Georgia. He was simply too much of an embarrassment to the presidency.

I think many of us have diminished the Holy Spirit to be some kind of Billy Carter caricature. We're afraid He'll act like a redneck poltergeist and sabotage the spiritual reputations we've worked so hard to establish. I mean, good night, what if He starts making a bunch of loud, windy noises around our non-Christian friends? What if we're enjoying a nice meal at a fancy restaurant and He makes flaming tongues shoot out of our mouths like a bananas Foster gone bad? The Holy Spirit definitely has the potential to embarrass us.

Theologian, pastor, and author Dr. Sinclair Ferguson astutely expounded on our misunderstanding of the Holy Spirit in his book about the third Person of the Trinity, *The Holy Spirit*:

> For while his *work* has been recognized, the Spirit *himself* remains to many Christians an anonymous, faceless aspect of the divine being. Even the title "Holy Spirit" evokes a different gamut of emotions from those expressed in response to the titles of "Father" and "Son."[1]

A SCENIC POINT ON THE ACTS JOURNEY

Remarkably, what with all the probability for awkwardness and denominational fisticuffs, immediately before His dramatic exit into glory, Jesus introduced the Holy Spirit as the indwelling empowerment we need: "But you will receive power when the Holy Spirit has come upon you" (Acts 1:8 ESV).

And while the next chapter of Acts unfolds like the Spirit's debutant party, He's actually been around from the very beginning. The exact moniker "Holy Spirit" is mentioned in three places in the Old Testament—Psalm 51:11, Isaiah 63:10, and Isaiah 63:11—but more common names for Him, like the "Spirit of God," the "Spirit of the Lord," the "Spirit of the Living God," or "My Spirit" are woven throughout the Old Testament.

The Holy Spirit was actively present in Creation:

The earth was empty and had no form. Darkness covered the ocean, and God's Spirit was moving over the water. (Genesis 1:2 NCV)

He was a catalyst among Moses and the Israelites in the wilderness:

Now two men remained in the camp, one named Eldad, and the other named Medad, and the Spirit rested on them. They were among those registered, but they had not gone out to the tent, and so they prophesied in the camp. And a young man ran and told Moses, "Eldad and Medad are prophesying in the camp." And Joshua the son of Nun, the assistant of Moses from his youth, said, "My lord Moses, stop them." But Moses said to him, "Are you jealous for my sake? Would that all the LORD's people were prophets, that the LORD would put his Spirit on them!" (Numbers 11:26–29 ESV)

His presence deeply convicted David, the teenage sling-shot sensation who went on to become the second king of

Israel, when David got jiggy with Bathsheba while she was
still married to Uriah the Hittite:

> *Create in me a clean heart, O God,*
> *and renew a right spirit within me.*
> *Cast me not away from your presence,*
> *and take not your Holy Spirit from me.*
> *(Psalm 51:10–11 ESV)*

And later on in the Psalter (all 150 psalms were originally
written as songs, so I like to think of that wonderful book in
the middle of the Bible as God's iPod playlist), David raves
about the comfort he receives from the constant compan-
ionship of the Holy Spirit:

> *Is there anyplace I can go to avoid your Spirit?*
> *to be out of your sight?*
> *If I climb to the sky, you're there!*
> *If I go underground, you're there!*
> *If I flew on morning's wings*
> *to the far western horizon,*
> *You'd find me in a minute—*
> *you're already there waiting!*
> *Then I said to myself, "Oh, he even sees me in the dark!*
> *At night I'm immersed in the light!"*
> *It's a fact: darkness isn't dark to you;*
> *night and day, darkness and light, they're all the same*
> *to you. (Psalm 139:7–12 THE MESSAGE)*

So while the Holy Spirit gets a lot of press in the book of Acts, it's important for us to remember this is not His first rodeo:

> When the day of Pentecost came, they were all together in one place. Suddenly a noise like a strong, blowing wind came from heaven and filled the whole house where they were sitting. They saw something like flames of fire that were separated and stood over each person there. They were all filled with the Holy Spirit, and they began to speak different languages by the power the Holy Spirit was giving them.
>
> There were some religious Jews staying in Jerusalem who were from every country in the world. When they heard this noise, a crowd came together. They were all surprised, because each one heard them speaking in his own language. They were completely amazed at this. They said, "Look! Aren't all these people that we hear speaking from Galilee? Then how is it possible that we each hear them in our own languages? We are from different places: Parthia, Media, Elam, Mesopotamia, Judea, Cappadocia, Pontus, Asia, Phrygia, Pamphylia, Egypt, the areas of Libya near Cyrene, Rome (both Jews and those who had become Jews), Crete, and Arabia. But we hear them telling in our own languages about the great things God has done!" They were all amazed and confused, asking each other, "What does this mean?"

But others were making fun of them, saying, "They have had too much wine." (Acts 2:1–13 NCV)

Wowzers. Although it wasn't His debutant party, you have to admit the Holy Spirit made a pretty dramatic entrance here. It was complete with the special effects of wind and fire, which are both symbolically revelatory—wind is a powerful, invisible force and fire is a powerful, purifying force. I can only imagine the collective wide-eyed stares and windblown coiffures the Holy Spirit's arrival caused.

Now, *a lot* of people were at this particular shindig. Pentecost—or "Feast of Weeks"—originally began as a harvest festival, but by the time of Jesus' earthly ministry it had evolved into a day commemorating God giving Moses the law on top of Mount Sinai. So it was a massive celebration. It was the second-most-significant holiday on the Jewish calendar, which meant workers got paid vacation days, kids got out of school, and women clogged the malls shopping for new outfits for weeks prior to the big event. People made the pilgrimage from all over the civilized world—Luke lists both Jews and Gentiles from at least fifteen nations in attendance—to Jerusalem to celebrate. Not unlike the World Cup. Or the Super Bowl. Or Mardi Gras. Or the semi-annual shoe sale at Nordstrom.

The ethnic barriers that likely existed at the beginning of this international gathering quickly dissipated when the disciples were filled with the power of the Holy Spirit and spoke in tongues. The original Greek word used here in Acts 2 for "tongues" is *xenolalia,* which refers to a known language. That means all these different people groups, from all these different countries, who spoke completely different dialects (if not completely different languages) heard about the unconditional, redemptive love of God in their native tongue. The two declarative promises Jesus made in Acts 1 showed up in His followers' lives fast:

> But *you will receive power* when the Holy Spirit has come
> upon you, and *you will be my witnesses* in Jerusalem and
> in all Judea and Samaria, and to the end of the earth.
> (Acts 1:8 ESV, emphasis mine)

ARE YOU WILLING TO RISK RECEIVING AND WIELDING MORE SPIRITUAL POWER?

Can you imagine being in a foreign country where you couldn't understand a word people were speaking around you, and then suddenly, in a flash, you were able to speak and understand everything fluently?

My friend Megan can. I met Megan the day after I met Missy, in a small town called Gressier not far from where my daughter was born. Megan moved there in her early twenties, soon after her college graduation, because she sensed God telling her to. She hadn't been a follower of Christ for very long at that point, but she was already radically obedient. Some might even call her crazy obedient because Megan moved to Haiti not knowing where she was going to live, what exactly God was calling her to do, and without speaking a word of Creole.

She said the first few months were really hard. She'd been a cheerleader in college but was now living in a hut without running water or electricity. She'd been surrounded by friends in the States but was now utterly alone. She'd graduated with honors but now was having a hard time forming simple sentences. So she got into the habit of hiking up the highest hill in Gressier most days to pray. One day she came across two little girls who were in obvious distress, probably child slaves called *restaveks* who'd been mistreated by their owner. Megan stopped to try and assist them, and it broke their dam of despair. A torrent of words she couldn't understand released from the girls. Megan told me she was so frustrated because while she believed God had brought her to Haiti to help people, the fact that she couldn't speak or understand Creole left her as the one who felt helpless. So she prayed an audacious prayer asking God to give her a way to help those precious girls, and in a flash she was able to speak and understand Creole fluently.

We were hiking up that same hill—toward the school that Megan Boudreaux and her team have since built through her incredible ministry Respire Haiti (the rest of her miraculous story can be found in her book, *Miracle on Voodoo Mountain*)—when she shared that story. No drama. No spotlight. No PowerPoint. Just two chicks trudging up a steep dirt trail in oppressive heat when I said, "I'm trying to learn Creole so I can communicate with Missy, but I'm having a hard time picking it up. How long did it take you to learn?" Tears were mingling with the perspiration streaking my dusty face by the time she finished and I couldn't help asking, "Megan, do you realize you experienced a modern Pentecost?" With remarkably less sweat and gasping, she replied softly, "Yeah, I guess I did."

In Megan's story, the supernatural "tongues" God gave enabled her to share compassion, medical assistance, food, and ultimately the unconditional love and living hope of Jesus Christ with two little girls. In the disciples' story of Acts 2, the supernatural "tongues" God gave them at Pentecost enabled them to share the unconditional love and living hope of Jesus Christ with those who were lost. In both cases the real miracle was not in the dramatic manifestation but in the message. When tongues are generated by the Holy Spirit, it is a powerfully redemptive gift. It doesn't hurt; it heals. It doesn't confuse; it clarifies. And it always, *always*, leads to Jesus.

Unfortunately there's a fly in the ointment because *glossalia* is another Greek word that's translated into "tongues" in our English Bibles. It's found in 1 Corinthians 14 and it refers to ecstatic speech rather than a known language. Some brilliant theologians, wonderful pastors, Christian leaders, and committed Christ-followers think the only proper manifestation of tongues is when it occurred as *xenolalia*—a known language. And they believe it only occurred at the event of Pentecost in Acts 2, that it is no longer a valid sign or gift of the Holy Spirit. The term for that doctrinal view is *cessationist* because it asserts that supernatural tongues have ceased.

Yet scads of other brilliant theologians, wonderful pastors, Christian leaders, and committed Christ-followers assert than supernatural tongues is still a relevant spiritual gift. Many believe that *xenolalia* occurs in modern culture.

Another widely held viewpoint is that *glossalia*—ecstatic speech, often called "speaking in tongues"—is a valid outward manifestation of the indwelling presence of the Holy Spirit and is helpful for encouragement in corporate worship (typically with an "interpretation" by a second person). They believe it also gives more power, wisdom, and intimacy with God when practiced in personal worship.

Those are just the most common dissenting views on the issue of tongues. The total variation of dissenting opinions outnumbers the drink choices at Starbucks. If you're curious, I am not a cessationist. I was, but God spanked the self-righteousness I had about this subject out of me *hard*. After several decades of study and prayer, I now believe that *one* of the gifts of the Holy Spirit is the manifestation of supernatural tongues.

However, I also think that when speaking in tongues is positioned as a sort of merit badge or bragging right for "enlightened" believers, we've missed the whole point. Because whether we're speaking a known dialect, an ecstatic one, or simply mangling the king's English with a strong Southern accent, our *language*—in word, attitude, and deed—should always lead others to the unconditional love and living hope of Jesus Christ. Anything else, as Paul so wisely said in 1 Corinthians, is just noise: "If I speak in the tongues of men and of angels, but have not love, I am a noisy gong or a clanging cymbal (1 Corinthians 13:1 ESV).

The following old, familiar adage still strikes a deep chord with me: "As followers of Christ we must be more consumed with the Giver than the gifts He blesses us with." Therefore, if the supernatural doesn't impact the way we live in the natural—if it doesn't deepen our love for God and the people He's called us into relationship with—then it really is just bells and whistles.

The New Testament English title "Holy Spirit" comes from the Greek words *pneuma* (spirit) and *haigon* (holy).

The Holy Spirit is also referred to as the *paraklētos* in the original Greek version of New Testament literature, which literally means "called to one's side." *Paraklētos* is translated into several different terms in our English Bibles including: *helper* (ESV, NASB), *counselor* (NIV), and *comforter* (KJV). See John 14:12-17; 15:26-27 and 16:7-8 for sample *paraklētos* passages.

"Pentecost" is the New Testament title for the "Festival of Weeks" or *Shavot,* which is the Hebrew word for "weeks." The ceremonial law in Leviticus 23:16 instructs the Israelites to count seven weeks from the end of Passover to this high holy day. That specified time period of seven weeks is also where the English word *Pentecost* came from because it's a transliteration of the Greek word *pentekostos,* meaning "fifty"—the approximate number of days in seven weeks.[2]

Even though the "Spirit of sonship" is used only once in Scripture to describe the Holy Spirit (Romans 8:15), John Calvin insisted that it should still be His title.[3]

The Old Testament Hebrew word for "spirit"—*ruach*—and the New Testament Greek word for "spirit"—*pneuma*—are onomatopoeic terms. Much like the way a cartoonist would doodle the word "whack!" above a boxer's punch landing on his opponent's jaw, this means the sound the word makes when it's said conveys its basic definition. In this case, that definition is "the expulsion of wind or air in motion." Thus, the biblical words used for the Holy Spirit express in the most fundamental way that He is the breath of life![4]

WHEN PUSH COMES TO SHOVE
AND RISK BECOMES REALITY

A few nights ago, Missy and I were sitting in a sticky booth at her favorite Mexican restaurant where she'd just eaten a cheese quesadilla twice the size of her head. She said, "Mama, can I sit wid chu?" This really means, "May I sit on your lap?" I replied, "Of course, honey," so she bounced to my side, leaned against me, and sighed dramatically. Then she patted her tummy and proclaimed with delighted satisfaction, "I so happy, Mama . . . I full!" Regardless of what your personal view is regarding the specific gift of tongues, I think the real treasure in this potentially polarizing passage is found at the beginning of verse four: "They were all filled" (Acts 2:4 NCV).

Like my baby with a bellyful of melted Monterey Jack, the disciples felt full, completely satisfied by the Spirit of the Living God. I believe this is the best gift in the Holy Spirit's prize closet—a deep sense of belonging to the family of God. A spirit of sonship. The security of divine adoption. The empowering realization that we have the right to call God "Dad":

> The Spirit you received does not make you slaves, so that you live in fear again; rather, the Spirit you received brought about your adoption to sonship. And by him we cry, "Abba, Father." (Romans 8:15 NIV)

Which begs the question, do you feel spiritually full? Are you satisfied in your relationship with Jesus? If not, maybe it's time for you to take the risk of asking the Holy Spirit to crash your party.

Exactly one month ago tonight I was lying in a twin bed next to Missy at her orphanage in Haiti wondering what finally bringing her home to TN was going to be like after two long years in the adoption process. Thousands of smiles, hundreds of belly laughs, multiple doctor visits, some tears, and one overflowed toilet later, I can honestly say the past four weeks have far exceeded my hopes and dreams. I would do it all over again a thousand times if need be. #thankYouJesus

(Instagram post from May 2014)

THREE

Checkered Pasts Can

Make Incredible Preachers

The journey to become Missy's mama started when I was seventeen years old, when Cindy Whelchel—my best friend in high school—and I led our youth group Bible study through the theme of adoption in Scripture. We made a pact to adopt babies that no one else wanted when we grew up. We were as sincere as we knew how to be when we made that solemn promise, while wearing matching pink Izods and flipping our Farrah Fawcett–inspired hair wings in 1981. We were walking in the light of all the revelation we had as perky, mostly devout teenage followers of Jesus. We had no idea Cindy would marry Peter after college, that they would struggle with infertility and then go on to adopt two beautiful children. Nor did we imagine that I'd still be single at fifty. I often tease and say my husband won't stop to ask for directions.

Frankly, being unmarried is the main reason I pondered

adoption for so long but never seriously pursued it. I grew up in the Waltons era, so the idea of having a child without a dad was pretty foreign to me. I think every child deserves two loving parents. But I attended a breakout session at a missions conference ten years ago and heard a speaker talk about the 147 *million* orphans in the world who are languishing in desperate situations in Third World countries with a slim-to-none shot at survival. She described the thousands of documented orphans here in America who are unwanted or about to age-out of foster care and how they don't have much hope for the future either unless someone steps up and fights for them. That's when the embers of the fire that had been lit two decades before began to stir. I found myself wondering, *You know, for kids like that who don't have anybody to love them, maybe an older, verbose, unmarried chick with a strong Southern accent, chemically dependent hair, and a guacamole addiction could work? I mean, if the choice is between me or life on the streets or even death, I just might be the better option!*

I drove home from the missions conference with James's admonition ringing in my ears: "Pure and genuine religion in the sight of God the Father means caring for orphans and widows in their distress" (James 1:27 NLT). The conversation in my head about this seemingly crazy idea grew more animated, *Okay, it sure doesn't sound like God's saying only married people with robust 401Ks have the assignment to take care of orphans in their distress. I'm pretty sure that verse is for the body of Christ. Which means maybe this scary excitement bubbling up in me that feels kind of like the start of a stomach virus could be the conviction of the Holy Spirit.* After a week or so of wrestling with what turned out *not* to be a stomach virus, I decided to call a social worker I'd met at church and begin some preliminary adoption paperwork. I also decided to share my budding hope with four girls I trusted from Bible study to ask them to pray with me as I began walking toward the riskiest decision I'd ever made. I wasn't ready to rent a billboard or anything, but I thought seeking counsel from a small circle of Christian friends was a smart thing to do while sticking my toe in the adoption pond.

Three of them gave me big teary hugs and an enthusiastic thumbs up. But one of them gave me a thin smile and asked if I'd be willing to meet her for coffee later. If you're wincing while reading this, your intuition is correct. I learned the hard way that when a rigid, religious "friend" wearing crop pants and toting a Bible clad in a personalized, quilted cover asks to chat with you privately in a condescending sing-song voice, you might want to bring a backup friend for support. A couple of days later, she clubbed my baby seal of a dream into a coma. She informed me that since I'd been sexually molested as a child, I wasn't good mom material. That even though I'd had extensive counseling, I probably still had toxic residue left over from the abuse and was therefore likely to spill icky emotional stuff on an unsuspecting child. She wrapped up her closing argument with another thin smile and this observation, "You know,

Lisa, it's understandable that you're lonely. Why don't you just go to the Humane Society and get another dog because you're so good with pets?"

I wish I could tell you I had the wisdom and spiritual maturity to realize that while Jesus might say "No" or "Wait" in response to my desire to adopt, He would *never* tell me I wasn't good enough to be a parent. I also wish I could tell you that I leaned across the table, took Negative Nancy's hand and said, "I'm so sorry for the places you've been wounded." Because obviously that kind of shriveled fruit comes from a tree that's suffered a devastating drought somewhere along the way. But I didn't. I just sat there stunned, paralyzed by a volley of accusations seasoned with just enough truth to be palatable. It would take seven more years before I was brave enough to limp toward the risky dream of adoption again.

Satan's strategy is effective because he sprinkles his poisonous brew with just enough veracity that we'll swallow it. Case in point, that old snake never throws me off course by saying, "Lisa, you're a woman of few words and a shockingly high metabolism." Nope. I'd recognize that lie from at least a mile away. But when he weaves in excerpts from the shameful chapters of my past, those ugly whispers have the power to make me pause. Somewhere in the core of my all-too-human heart, I'm afraid my former life could sabotage the abundant future Jesus promised those of us who put our hope in Him.

Which is why Peter will always be one of the biblical personalities I resonate with most. His story is at the top of my favorite list because the trajectory of his life proves that our mistake-strewn pasts don't dictate our glorious, God-authored destinies!

A SCENIC POINT ON THE ACTS JOURNEY

Immediately after the Holy Spirit swept through the Pentecost party with hurricane force winds, fiery special effects, and jaw-dropping linguistic miracles, Peter stood up to preach to this crowd of thousands. The multitude wasn't comprised of ten- or twenty-thousand mild-mannered churchgoers sitting in pews with their hands calmly clasped in front of them either. Nope, this was an unruly mob on the verge of panic. Surely they were gaping in shock and wonder. Perhaps some were even shrieking, and still others may have fainted as a result of the emotionally evocative, supernatural occurrences they'd just witnessed. But Pete doesn't appear to be intimidated when he clears his throat and begins to bellow the first sermon of his pastoral career in this less-than-conducive environment:

> Then Peter stepped forward with the eleven other apostles and shouted to the crowd, "Listen carefully, all of you, fellow Jews and residents of Jerusalem! Make no mistake about this. These people are not drunk, as some of you are assuming. Nine o'clock in the morning is much too early for that. No, what you see was predicted long ago by the prophet Joel:

'In the last days,' God says,
'I will pour out my Spirit upon all people.
Your sons and daughters will prophesy.
Your young men will see visions,
and your old men will dream dreams.
In those days I will pour out my Spirit
even on my servants—men and women alike—
and they will prophesy.
And I will cause wonders in the heavens above
and signs on the earth below—
blood and fire and clouds of smoke.
The sun will become dark,
and the moon will turn blood red
before that great and glorious day of the LORD *arrives.*
But everyone who calls on the name of the LORD
will be saved.'

"People of Israel, listen! God publicly endorsed Jesus the Nazarene by doing powerful miracles, wonders, and signs through him, as you well know. But God knew what would happen, and his prearranged plan was carried out when Jesus was betrayed. With the help of lawless Gentiles, you nailed him to a cross and killed him. But God released him from the horrors of death and raised him back to life, for death could not keep him in its grip. King David said this about him:

'I see that the LORD *is always with me.*
I will not be shaken, for he is right beside me.

> *No wonder my heart is glad,*
> *and my tongue shouts his praises!*
> *My body rests in hope.*
> *For you will not leave my soul among the dead*
> *or allow your Holy One to rot in the grave.*
> *You have shown me the way of life,*
> *and you will fill me with the joy of your presence.'*

"Dear brothers, think about this! You can be sure that the patriarch David wasn't referring to himself, for he died and was buried, and his tomb is still here among us. But he was a prophet, and he knew God had promised with an oath that one of David's own descendants would sit on his throne. David was looking into the future and speaking of the Messiah's resurrection. He was saying that God would not leave him among the dead or allow his body to rot in the grave.

"God raised Jesus from the dead, and we are all witnesses of this. Now he is exalted to the place of highest honor in heaven, at God's right hand. And the Father, as he had promised, gave him the Holy Spirit to pour out upon us, just as you see and hear today. For David himself never ascended into heaven, yet he said,

> *'The LORD said to my Lord,*
> *"Sit in the place of honor at my right hand*
> *until I humble your enemies,*
> *making them a footstool under your feet."'*

"So let everyone in Israel know for certain that God has made this Jesus, whom you crucified, to be both Lord and Messiah!" (Acts 2:14–36 NLT)

This first of two Petrine speeches (the fancy, formal classification of Peter's monologues in the book of Acts) is so packed full of amazing stuff it's like drinking from a fire hose of grace. In fact, we get to tear the wrapping paper off one gift before Pete even opens his mouth, because when Luke describes him as standing up (verse 14), the original Greek verb indicates not only the physical posture of rising, but a "standing up" in character.[1] In other words, the very same best-friend-who-became-a-weasel, who wimped out in the homestretch before Jesus was crucified, now bravely faces a massive, unruly crowd as the de facto leader of the apostles. Which, when you stop and think about it, is basically next to impossible.

I mean, really.

Apostle of Jesus Christ: This biblical distinction typically refers to the twelve men handpicked by Jesus to accompany and assist Him in His earthly ministry (Luke 6:13; 9:10); however, this term was also used to describe Paul, who was directly commissioned by a resurrected Jesus after He blinded him on the road to Damascus (Acts 9), Barnabas, Andronicus and Junias (Romans 16:7), two unnamed Christ-followers (2 Corinthians 8:23), Epaphroditus (Philippians 2:25), and Paul's co-laborers, Silas and Timothy (1 Thessalonians 2:7).

That'd be like finding out on Easter weekend that your fiancé slept with your would-be-maid-of-honor and then believing him when he recites his vows to be your loving and faithful husband, in plenty and want, in joy and in sorrow, in sickness and in health, as long as we both shall live at your Memorial Day weekend wedding seven weeks later.

I'm. So. Sure.

I can almost hear the snickers in the white-tulle-draped sanctuary now. Only an idiot would believe somebody could make such a complete 180-degree turn in his moral compass in that short of a time period! A sane bride-to-be would've canceled the ceremony and flushed his ring down the toilet. Or sold it on eBay and bought cute shoes for a solo trip to Tahiti.

But the miraculous unlikelihood of it all is exactly Luke's point.

Remember that a week or so after Pete vigorously and vulgarly denied he knew Jesus and the Prince of Peace was nailed to a tree on a hill outside of Jerusalem, the resurrected

Jesus appeared to Peter and forgave him for his betrayal (John 21). And remember that Jesus—who *knew* Peter would fumble the ball on the first yard line—still commissioned him to be the very rock He was going to build the early church on (Matthew 16:18). Peter obviously believed His Savior's mercy and commissioning were sincere because, out of eleven apostles who were present at Pentecost, he's the one who bravely chose to accept the challenge of addressing the throng.

I think Peter was ready and willing to articulate the truth of the gospel in that hyped-up environment because he'd been so recently and radically transformed by it. He was the Holy Spirit's hand-picked show-and-tell on that red-letter day because only the power of the Holy Spirit could raise a man from Benedict-Arnold-like behavior to Billy-Graham-like boldness!

Before a word even fell out of his forgiven pie-hole, Peter proved God's redemptive mercy is so all-encompassing that it not only pardons sinners, but it gives us a role in His kingdom purposes. In the wild and wooly world of amazing grace, ex-cons who served time for embezzling are the same ones God chooses to run banks! And hopeful, single mamas-to-be with knocking knees and fickle faith don't have to settle for Labrador Retrievers with bladder control problems.

Pete goes on to recite a prophetic passage from Joel that illustrates how the outpouring of the Holy Spirit ushered in the Messianic era. Then he lets loose with his first zinger:

People of Israel, listen to these words: Jesus from Nazareth
was a very special man. God clearly showed this to you
by the miracles, wonders, and signs he did through Jesus.
You all know this, because it happened right here among
you. Jesus was given to you, and with the help of those
who don't know the law, *you* put him to death by nailing
him to a cross. (Acts 2:22–23 NCV, emphasis mine)

You put him to death! Yikers, talk about a buzz kill. Can
you imagine how well that indictment went over with this
crowd of Mardi Gras revelers who'd just observed enough
supernatural fireworks to make them frantically text their
mental health counselors? Surely somebody groaned, grabbed
their chest, and squealed in protest, "Stop! Enough already!
I don't even know this Jesus dude you're talking about, plus I
forgot to take my Lipitor this morning and all this brouhaha
is shooting my blood pressure through the roof!"

In all fairness, Pete's remarks do seem to be a tad over-
reaching here because many in this Pentecost crowd weren't
even in Jerusalem a month and a half before when the Son of
God was set up by Caiaphas and hung on a cross outside the
city. Technically this means they weren't *really* responsible
for that very first Good Friday, right? Wrong. The point
Peter's making in his inaugural address is that to be human
is to be a sinner (see also Romans 3:23). Therefore every
single one of us who takes up space on this planet is per-
sonally responsible for the sacrificial, propitiatory death of
Jesus Christ. We are all guilty as charged.

ARE YOU WILLING TO RISK THE ON-GOING ACT OF REPENTANCE?

I bet the timbre of Peter's voice softened when he used the affectionate term "dear brothers" (Acts 2:29 NLT)—an inclusive Greek term that encompassed the chicks in the crowd too—before he launched into another Old Testament passage (Psalm 16) to illustrate the fact that Jesus didn't stay dead like their hero King David. My guess is most of the folks within earshot of Pete's sermon were really leaning in now. At the very least, they were curious about what in the world he was going to say next. And that's when he swings for the fence: "Let all the house of Israel therefore know for certain that God has made him both Lord and Christ, *this Jesus* whom *you* crucified" (Acts 2:36 ESV, emphasis mine).

Just in case anybody missed it the first time he accused them of murdering the Messiah, Peter puts it in neon lights on the marque: *You killed this Jesus.* This Jesus, the One who is both Lord *and* Christ. The first apostolic speech inspired the beginning of the Apostle's Creed.

Disciple of Jesus Christ: anyone who follows the teachings of Jesus Christ.[2]

It's important to remember that prior to this moment in history "Lord" had been a title exclusively ascribed by Jews to Jehovah, the God of Israel, and "Christ" was a title exclusively used by Jews to describe the coming Messiah or "Anointed One." So Peter's assertion that *this* Jesus from Nazareth, which is akin to saying "John from the boondocks" since Jesus was a very common name in Hellenistic Jewish culture and Nazareth was a very dinky town, was the King of all kings as well as the divine Redeemer Yahweh had promised was a radical claim. And yet the Holy Spirit permeated Peter's words with such power that many recognized the indisputable truth to his outrageous claim and were pierced with guilt:

> Now when they heard this they were cut to the heart, and said to Peter and the rest of the apostles, "Brothers, what shall we do?" And Peter said to them, "Repent and be baptized every one of you in the name of Jesus Christ for the forgiveness of your sins, and you will receive the gift of the Holy Spirit. For the promise is for you and for your children and for all who are far off, everyone whom the Lord our God calls to himself." And with many other words he bore witness and continued to exhort them, saying, "Save yourselves from this crooked generation." So those who received his word were baptized, and there were added that day about three thousand souls. (Acts 2:37–41 ESV)

The idea of a Savior was so pervasive in Israel's history that the English transliterations of *Yeshua*, Joshua and Hosea, meaning "Jehovah is my salvation," were popular Jewish boy's names. In Greek, Joshua (or Hosea) becomes *Jesus*, a moniker that continues to be popular in modern day culture. Consider the proliferation of Jesus translations: *Jesus* (pronounced hey-suz) in Hispanic culture, *Salvador* ("Savior") in Brazilian culture, and *Salvatore* ("Savior") in Italian culture. The bottom line is the name Jesus is relatively common, but when you add His title, *Christ*, which means the "Anointed One" or "Messiah," His is the name above every other name.

It's one thing to feel guilty about doing something wrong, but it's a whole other thing to admit you're in the wrong and then be willing to do whatever it takes to get right. In spiritual terms it's called repentance. It's a costly, pride-shattering, 180-degree shift from self-centeredness to Christ-dependency. Peter was the poster child for it. So I think it's especially poignant that he gets to be the first New Testament preacher to witness thousands of others so overcome with repentance that they humbly hurled themselves at the feet of *this Jesus* . . . his Jesus.

Propitiation: the provision God made through the vicarious and expiatory sacrifice of Jesus Christ to deal with mankind's sin so that He could show mercy to the believing sinner in the removal and remission of his sins.[3] In other words, the perfect pacification for the sin that caused God's wrath.

WHEN PUSH COMES TO SHOVE AND RISK BECOMES REALITY

When I was first learning how to use the integrated Bluetooth phone system in my car, I was like a platypus on a treadmill—totally inept and out of my element. First of all, the whole thing seemed to have a mind of its own. I'd be cruising down the road, happily accompanying Alicia Keys, when suddenly I'd hear a faint disembodied voice in the distance saying, "Hello? Hello? Lisa?" Before I had time to figure out how to mute the music (which, according to the manual that came with the car, was supposed to happen automatically) the voice would get louder in pitch and demanding in tone, "Lisa? LISA? IS THAT YOU? TURN DOWN THE MUSIC SO I CAN HEAR YOU!"

Being jolted out of a New York state of mind is mild compared to what happened a few years ago. The Bluetooth troll who lives in my glove compartment redialed a nice woman named Sally (names have been changed to protect the innocent) immediately after we'd hung up, but I was gossiping with my passenger about how, in spite of her kindness, she bugged me because she always managed to rope me into helping with her workload which was negatively affecting mine. My friend nodded sympathetically and then launched into her own reasons for painting Sally in the naughty corner. We'd spent the better part of five minutes filleting our mutual acquaintance over her minor shortcomings when I heard the familiar sound that occurs whenever a call is dropped. I noticed the ominous blinking message, "Call with Sally ended," flashing on my fancy Bluetooth-enabled dashboard screen.

That's when I felt something similar to what Luke describes in Acts as being "cut to the heart." Or as *The Message* says, "cut to the quick." It's when the Holy Spirit made like a Wonder Twin and morphed into a bowling ball of conviction and settled in the pit of my stomach. Double ugh.

I knew immediately what I had to do. So after dropping off my other wincing and chastised friend, I called Sally again. Only this time it was on purpose. And based on the hurt in her voice, I knew she'd already heard the recording of our harsh commentary. I don't remember exactly what I said during that agonizing apology, but I do remember I didn't attempt to make any excuses. Not because I'm so gifted at repentance, but because it was impossible to refute what I'd done. My sin was recorded in Dolby stereo. If she'd wanted to, Sally could've saved my tacky trespass in a digital format on her hard drive. It was my very own Watergate. Thankfully

Sally has a generous heart and responded to my stammering, red-faced full disclosure with grace and understanding.

There's beauty in repentance, in recognizing that you desperately need absolution after blowing it big time. The sweet relief and liberating freedom that accompany being forgiven are so much bigger than the guilt that prompts the confession in the first place. Especially when being cut to the heart by our own culpability compels us to run toward Jesus. That kind of godly repentance unleashes an avalanche of divine compassion that not only cleanses the stain of guilt— the fact that we've *done* something wrong—but also the stain of shame—the feeling that we *are* something wrong.

One final thought: I think all too often we hear the word *repentance* in our heads uttered with a deep bass voice that comes off sounding punitive, like we're going to be sent to some stern, ethereal principal's office and paddled with a lightning bolt. But the truth is found in Romans 2:4, where it says God's kindness—His love—is what leads us to repentance. Love is the catalyst. Love leads the way. Responding to the unconditional love of Jesus Christ is what transformed Peter and it's what ultimately launched the early church in the book of Acts.

Here's the deal, y'all. God. Already. Knows. His people are a hot, sinful mess, so when we simply acknowledge that and repent, He's waiting with open arms. We don't have to justify ourselves because Jesus already did that on the cross. So the risk of repentance doesn't lead to punishment—it leads to the unilateral forgiveness and unconditional affection of our Creator Redeemer. Vegas only wished it had a payout that humongous.

● I saw my future today and realized it will include hundreds of hours sitting in miniature plastic chairs covered w/globs of sticky stuff. And hordes of shrieking children. And terrible-tasting pizza. And other parents wearily scrolling their iPhones, too exhausted to chat. And I couldn't help but smile in spite of the mild horror of it all. #7weekshomefromHaiti #middleagedmiracle #onlyGod

(Instagram post from June 2, 2014)

FOUR

What's Mine Is Yours

A few months ago I was signing books at a conference and noticed a woman hovering about twenty feet away. Every time I looked up, she glanced nervously in my direction. As soon as I could, I walked over and introduced myself. She was wearing a waitress uniform that had seen better days and said that she'd come to the event straight from her morning shift at a pancake house. I wasn't surprised when she said she identified with the stories I'd shared about some of my friends at The Next Door (a faith-based recovery program for women who are addicted to drugs and alcohol that I volunteer at in downtown Nashville). She went on to describe how she'd been addicted to meth for six years and had gotten clean just two months before the conference.

She explained that what I'd said about Jesus loving broken people and that our pasts don't determine our destiny really blessed her. Then she pressed a crumpled twenty-dollar bill in my hand and said, "I wish I had more to give you, but please take this and use it for gas so you can go more

places and tell more people like me that Jesus loves them."
It was obvious she needed the money more than I did, so I
replied, "Oh wow, thank you so much, but your encouragement is enough of a gift. Please keep this." I tried to press
the bill back into her closed fist. When a look of disappoint-
ment washed across her face, I immediately regretted my
inappropriate response. She leaned closer and whispered,
"Please, I really want to help," so I accepted the bill with
the gravitas a sacrificial gift like that deserves, hugged her
for a long time, and said, "Thank you very much; you've
helped me more than you know."

The lesson God engraved on my heart that day was
while I didn't necessarily need the money, she needed to give
it. The exchange itself—both the giving and the receiving—
illustrates a key characteristic of Christian community.
To open-handedly bless others from the riches God has so
generously given us and to open-handedly receive blessings
from others binds believers together in an interdependent,
Jesus-and-others-oriented web of grace.

A SCENIC POINT ON THE ACTS JOURNEY

The first notes of the early church—our spiritual ancestors—were a gorgeous symphony of that kind of generosity.
These Holy-Spirit-fueled folks were so gifted at giving they
made Santa look bush league:

And all the believers lived in a wonderful harmony, holding everything in common. They sold whatever they owned and pooled their resources so that each person's need was met.

They followed a daily discipline of worship in the Temple followed by meals at home, every meal a celebration, exuberant and joyful, as they praised God. People in general liked what they saw. Every day their number grew as God added those who were saved. (Acts 2:43–47 THE MESSAGE)

Good night, what an awesome neighborhood! They were relational and caring: "all the believers lived in wonderful harmony, holding everything in common." They were devoted to God and each other: "they followed a daily discipline of worship in the Temple followed by meals at home." Plus, they were fun to be around: "every meal a celebration, exuberant and joyful." It's no wonder their church was growing like a weed! What started out as 120 believers at the beginning of Acts (1:15) quickly swelled to 3,120 following Pete's first sermon (Acts 2:41), and then exploded to 8,120 congregants while Pete was being dragged off to jail as a result of his second sermon (Acts 4:4). Not unlike that old barn on the edge of town where Kevin Bacon and his rhythmic friends liked to boogie in *Footloose*, the First Ever Bapticostal Church of Acts was *the* place to hang out in the heady spiritual culture that existed after the resurrection and ascension of Jesus.

And boy-oh-boy were these New Testament hoofers in sync:

> Now the full number of those who believed were of one heart and soul, and no one said that any of the things that belonged to him was his own, but they had everything in common. And with *great power* the apostles were giving their testimony to the resurrection of the Lord Jesus, and *great grace* was upon them all. There was not a needy person among them, for as many as were owners of lands or houses sold them and brought the proceeds of what was sold and laid it at the apostles' feet, and it was distributed to each as any had need. Thus Joseph, who was also called by the apostles Barnabas (which means son of encouragement), a Levite, a native of Cyprus, sold a field that belonged to him and brought the money and laid it at the apostles' feet. (Acts 4:32–37 ESV; emphasis mine)

Their spiritual tango of sacrificial giving and real relationship demonstrated great power (from the Greek word *dynamis*, which means "force or boldness") and great grace (from the Greek word *charis*, which means "unmerited favor") to the watching world. Lots of people began taking note of this crazy crew who actually seemed to be walking the "love the LORD with all your heart, soul, mind and strength, and love your neighbor as you love yourself" talk. They were causing quite the sensation.

On December 2, 2012, a twenty-four-year-old Spanish

athlete named Ivan Fernandez Anaya finished second in a cross-country race in Burlada, Spain. But it was a sensational finish. According to bystanders, Anaya was running behind Abel Mutai, a Kenyan athlete who had won a bronze medal at the London Olympics. Suddenly Mutai slowed down, about 10 meters short of the finish line. Anaya could've easily surged ahead and won the race, but he realized Mutai—who didn't speak Spanish and couldn't understand the crowd that was urging him on—mistakenly thought he'd completed the course. So Anaya stopped and guided his competitor across the line, allowing him to rightfully finish first.[1]

Anaya's intentional "loss" made headlines around the world and won him scads of new Twitter followers and Facebook fans. People were attracted to his selflessness. I think deep down in the human heart, we all long to be treated that way. In fact, the Bible makes it clear that we're divinely wired for real, benevolent, reciprocal relationships:

> Then God said, "Let us make man in *our* image, after *our* likeness. And let them have dominion over the fish of the sea and over the birds of the heavens and over the livestock and over all the earth and over every creeping thing that creeps on the earth."
>
> So God created man in his own image,
> in the image of God he created him;
> male and female he created them.
> (Genesis 1:26–27 ESV, emphasis mine)

God is an *us*, a Trinitarian Redeemer in perfect relation-ship with Himself—God the Father, God the Son, and God the Holy Spirit. And since He created us in His image, the blueprint for relational unity is in our DNA. We were made for that kind of *koinonia* . . . for authentic fellowship.

> The Greek term *koinonia* (pronounced coy-no-knee-ah) means "fellowship, the close association between persons, emphasizing what is common between them: by extension: participation, sharing, contribu-tion, gift, the outcome of such close relationships."[2] In the biblical text it's first used in Acts 2:42.

We were created for deep connections with relatively safe people who are willing to carry us to rooftops, whip out a saw, cut a hole, and then lower us to Jesus when we need healing, like a band of brothers did for their paralyzed friend in Mark 2:1–5.

We were created for deep connections with relatively safe people who are willing to sacrifice their own comfort and security for our well-being, like Jonathan did for David in spite of his whacko dad in 1 Samuel 20.

We were created for deep connections with relatively safe people who are willing to walk alongside us even when we're not the best company, like Ruth stuck by her bitter mother-in-law, Naomi, in Ruth 1:1–18.

Deep connections with relatively safe people mean we can count on a tribe to be cheering with us and for us, not because we necessarily deserve it, but because they claim us as theirs.

Whether you're Catholic or Protestant and regardless of our individual creeds and dogmas, all Christian churches can trace their roots back to this first New Testament congregation of Christ followers described in Acts 2. In spite of the vitriolic arguments over theology that exist now in the body of Christ—and have existed for thousands of years—we're all either "plants" or "splits" from that original community of faith.

Anglican bishop and theologian Lesslie Newbigin went so far as to claim that deep connections with relatively safe people can help us see Jesus bigger. He wrote, "The congregation is the hermeneutic of the Gospel."[3] In other words, we formulate our understanding of who our Redeemer is largely through the lens of relationships with other Christians. Of course, Jesus Himself put the cherry on top of the sundae of Christian community when He explained to an arrogant young Jewish lawyer that the entire law of God, which most orthodox Jews believe is contained in a detailed, pretty-much-impossible-to-keep list of 613 regulations, could be summed up by saying we are to love God and love others (Luke 10:25–28). Church was never intended to be an anemic two-hour, once-a-week assembly of well-dressed people. It was always supposed to be a powerful force for our good and God's glory.

Such was the kind of congregation described in the first few chapters of Acts. But of course, as fantastic as their first season of doing life together was, it wasn't glory. Theirs was an earthbound gathering, so there were bound to be a few weeds in the garden.

ARE YOU WILLING TO RISK THE GIVE-AND-TAKE OF REAL RELATIONSHIPS?

While researching Ivan Fernandez Anaya's amazing race, I found it really interesting that one person who didn't applaud his generous choice to step back and allow his confused opponent to receive the rightful victory was his coach. In fact, when a reporter questioned Anaya's coach about the event, he replied, it was "a gesture I myself wouldn't have made. I certainly would have taken advantage of it to win."[4]

Here's where I'm going with this: I think as much as we long to be in open-handed, open-hearted, generous giving-and-receiving relationships, we still lean toward protecting ourselves with clandestine I'll-take-advantage-of-whatever-I-can-to-win convictions. We're prone to operate with a scarcity mentality, as if we're secretly afraid that God's grace can somehow be depleted. We tend to believe that the more we give away, the less we'll end up with, so we piously fold a check and place it in the weekly offering plate, sponsor a kid or two through Third World relief organizations, or better still, weave our church's online giving program into conversations about technology (thereby implying that we're generous *and* hip), all the while withholding more than enough to ensure our comfort. We have the audacity to attempt to cheat on God!

Which is exactly the first noxious weed that cropped up in the early church:

> But there was a certain man named Ananias who, with his wife, Sapphira, sold some property. He brought part of the money to the apostles, claiming it was the full amount. With his wife's consent, he kept the rest.
>
> Then Peter said, "Ananias, why have you let Satan fill your heart? You lied to the Holy Spirit, and you kept some of the money for yourself. The property was yours to sell or not sell, as you wished. And after selling it, the money was also yours to give away. How could you do a thing like this? You weren't lying to us but to God!"
>
> As soon as Ananias heard these words, he fell to the floor and died. Everyone who heard about it was terrified. Then some young men got up, wrapped him in a sheet, and took him out and buried him.
>
> About three hours later his wife came in, not knowing

what had happened. Peter asked her, "Was this the price you and your husband received for your land?"

"Yes," she replied, "that was the price."

And Peter said, "How could the two of you even think of conspiring to test the Spirit of the Lord like this? The young men who buried your husband are just outside the door, and they will carry you out, too."

Instantly, she fell to the floor and died. When the young men came in and saw that she was dead, they carried her out and buried her beside her husband. Great fear gripped the entire church and everyone else who heard what had happened. (Acts 5:1–11 NLT)

The name Ananias means "God is gracious" and the name Sapphira signifies "beautiful."[5] This irony reminds me of Manny Yarboro, a 719-pound World Champion sumo wrestler from New Jersey whose nickname is "Tiny." Unfortunately the propensity to lie, cheat, steal, and behave like greedy little pigs didn't die along with this ancient couple. The body of Christ is still infected with stinkers.

Our smelly, scarcity mentality doesn't just impact church coffers either; it hardens the arteries of our communities and compromises the health of our relationships. When we wonder if someone else's receiving a big blessing—such as a raise, a good spouse, a beautiful home, a well-behaved-honor-roll-earning child, a healthy diagnosis, the praise of others—means less blessing for us, we swing wide the door to disunity. That's when we find ourselves smiling at other's good fortune to their face but frowning behind their backs. Or politely applauding their success in public but daydreaming about their comeuppance in private. Or even stooping low enough to sow seeds of doubt about the upright character of dear friends through small group gossip disguised as prayer requests.

Thankfully for us, you don't hear much any more about God zapping people into grease spots like He did Ananias and Sapphira. Even more praiseworthy, God's goodness doesn't fit on a pie chart. If someone else gets a big piece, that doesn't mean our slice inevitably gets smaller. It's more like an all-you-can-eat buffet. His grace and mercy don't run out—they're baked fresh every morning (Lamentations 3:23). We get to fill up our plates again and again and again, ad infinitum.

And not only is God's goodness inexhaustible, the Bible reveals He'll give us extra credit when we mirror His generosity:

> *One gives freely, yet grows all the richer;*
> *another withholds what he should give, and only suf-*
> *fers want."* (Proverbs 11:24 ESV)

So it stands to reason that the more generous we are with God and others, the wealthier we'll be. Mind you, we'll always have stinkers to deal with this side of heaven. And we're all going to get a bit banged up in community. But as the Skin Horse explains in the beautiful children's story *The Velveteen Rabbit*, the dings and dents and scrapes and scars are what put the *real* in relationship.

I read another book recently about how human vocal cords develop. Babies are incapable of speech and can only use their larynx for emergencies, not for language.[6] However, it's been scientifically documented that the sound an infant makes when in distress stimulates other people—including seemingly non-nurturing, collegiate men—to react and provide assistance. Even Darwinian researchers admit there's something legitimate—if not completely quantifiable—in the human organism that's uniquely created for connection. In light of this experiment, it might not be too much of a stretch to say our survival as a human race is dependent upon how well we learn to share.

WHEN PUSH COMES TO SHOVE AND RISK BECOMES REALITY

Five years ago, I lost both my stepfather and my closest friend of more than ten years. The losses knocked me off my feet. It's the first time in my life I literally had a hard time getting out of bed. One morning, I woke up and felt such crushing sadness that I took an Ambien in order to go back to sleep and not feel anything for another eight or nine hours. I wasn't suicidal; I didn't want to die. I just didn't want to slip into the deep crevasse of grief this loss had unearthed in my soul. I wanted to somehow catapult over the void or detour around it.

I'd never experienced depression before, at least not that I would admit to. I'd become adept at medicating with busyness. If sorrow was lurking around the corner of my heart, I'd go to work, putter in the garden, make a phone call, ride my motorcycle, clean the garage, or go to Bible study—*anything* to distract me from feeling sad.

But this time I got sucker-punched so hard I wasn't able to kick into self-defense mode. I just folded. After forty-five years of sunny optimism and self-reliance, I found myself unable to do anything but ache. And while I was lying there, still seeing white spots and reeling from the pain, I sensed God clearly say: *I'm going to walk with you down into the basement of your soul where the boogyman of fear lives. I'm going to sit with you in that dark, dank space until fear doesn't own you anymore. It's time for you to quit being afraid.* I responded to His tenderness with tears that lasted for six months.

Here's what I was so terrified of: being left emotionally alone. I was afraid that if someone—really *anyone*—with skin on didn't love me completely and forever, I couldn't make it. Now, I've spent a small fortune listening to licensed counselors and one, Lynn Husband, turned out to be a life-changing vessel of biblical wisdom, kind rebuke, consistent encouragement, and safe accountability. She and all the others will tell you I had a classic case of fear of abandonment. Because of several wounds that took place during my early and adolescent development—my dad leaving for another woman and her child; my parents' ensuing, acrimonious divorce; the emotional and sexual abuse I endured afterward—I had a difficult time trusting people. I struggled with feelings of shame and unworthiness. I sought the approval of everybody, especially men in authority. And I took too much responsibility for the well-being of friends and family members in order to establish my value so they wouldn't leave me. And they'd be right. I've been guilty of all those flaws and many, many more.

The indictment that was even harder to deal with was the growing realization that I'd basically been an emotional agnostic for decades. That while I love Jesus and have believed the Bible to be the authoritative Word of God for as long as I can remember, there was still part of me that refused to trust Jesus. To rest in the sufficiency of His unconditional, immutable love. At my very core, I wasn't positive He could sustain me. But I wasn't brave enough to really ponder any of this until I lost two people who meant the world to me but with whom I'd made a complete mess of things.

I withheld affection from one because I was afraid he'd hurt me again so badly I wouldn't recover. I held onto the other with a white-knuckled grip because I thought her acceptance could heal me. I completely blew it with both of them. My wall of self-protection and clench of desperation gave John Angel and my old friend authority and responsibility they didn't ask for. Or deserve. What they deserved was for me to reach out with compassion and loosen my grip with confidence. They needed me to be interdependent instead of codependent. But I wasn't—not until the eleventh hour anyway. This led to me standing over two graves, one literal and one figurative, filled with remorse.

We covered the concept of divine redemption when we talked about the restoration and transformation of Peter from world-class betrayer to first-class evangelist in chapter 3, but it's a concept I never tire of examining. Like a diamond, I love to hold the miracle of God's redemptive nature up to the light and watch brilliance bounce off its facets. It's precious to me because it means the One I didn't fully believe was enough to sustain me reached down into an awful pit I'd dug, lifted me out, slung me over His shoulder, and carried me to a new place. A place filled with mostly harmonious relationships with friends and family members who've been extraordinarily patient with me as I learn to give and receive better.

Four years after that near-fatal emotional crash, God gave me a passport to the glorious country of parenthood. He filled my world with the whispers and shouts and tears and giggles and endearments and pouts of a beautiful child named Missy who deserves a mama who will love her with open hands that don't push her away or pull her too tightly or put her on an altar where only God belongs. And don't think for a minute it's escaped my attention that the little girl He lovingly placed in my arms came from such difficult circumstances that she has some abandonment issues as well. Our Savior is the Author of second chances.

Whether in church or at home, true community—a place

where people are generous and glad and devoted to each other like the believers were at the beginning of Acts—is a rare and precious gift. And I've come to believe the only way we can attain that kind of intimacy is to adopt the fourth characteristic demonstrated by the early church, that is by first devoting ourselves to God. We must make Him the main source we draw from, because our Creator Redeemer is the only One with inexhaustible resources. He's the only One who has the capacity to be our power grid. When we plug ourselves into anyone else, there's bound to be a lost connection or a complete blackout.

However, when we work at placing the entirety of ourselves into God's perfect custody, we can freely enjoy rich life with others because our desire for unconditional love and acceptance is lying appropriately at His feet, not theirs. Of course, we can only walk in the light of the revelation we have today, so by tomorrow we'll have more emotional expectations to hurl at His throne. But the more we allow our crooked little hearts to be kept securely by Jesus, the more courage we'll have to dive into the deep water of real relationships. It's a milieu where every single one of us will have epic fails at some point or another. But it's a place incredibly worth the inherent peril because the only other option is untenable:

Love anything, and your heart will certainly be wrung and positively broken. If you want to make sure of keeping it intact, you must give your heart to no one, not even to an animal. Wrap it carefully round with hobbies and little luxuries; avoid all entanglements; lock it up safe in the casket or coffin of your selfishness. But in that casket—safe, dark, motionless, airless—it will change. It will not be broken; it will become unbreakable, impenetrable, irredeemable. The alternative to tragedy, or at least to the risk of tragedy, is damnation.[7]

Watching Missy run around and interact so comfortably with our extended family of faith tonight while we waited to welcome our dear friends "Uncle Kyle" @kylecooksey and "Aunt Lala" @laurabcooksey home for the first time with their three adopted kids was really sweet. I can hardly believe it's only been seven and a half weeks since I brought her home from Haiti and now her "cousins" are with their forever family too. I am once again amazed by the goodness of our God. His works are wonderful, I know that full well (Psalm 139:14). #onlyGod

(Instagram post from June 3, 2014, when Kyle and Laura brought their kids home)

FIVE

Loving More People, More

"It was the best of times, it was the worst of times." That phrase, penned by the incomparable Charles Dickens at the beginning of his novel *A Tale of Two Cities*, is arguably one of the most powerful lines in literature. Those twelve words beautifully describe the juxtaposition of rapture and rupture that mankind will regularly experience this side of glory. Like the quarter you blow your sales quota out of the water, right before your boss announces the company's been sold and there won't be any bonuses after all. Or the day you finally pay your car off but have a fender bender immediately afterward because you just had to text the good news to your BFF while driving. Then there's the week you're finally able to finish all of your Beth Moore homework, and Bible study is cancelled due to a plumbing emergency at church. Of course, there's probably going to be a year when you're bathing-suit-ready by Spring Break, and your husband proclaims at dinner that he's rented a condo in Colorado for a family ski vacation "since it's usually cold at the beach in March anyway!"

While the majority of motherhood has been far more glorious than I could've imagined, there has definitely been some groaning, some of which is due to the fact that Missy is HIV+. Like the time I took her to the first of what will likely be a lifetime of visits to Dr. Craig Wilson, a pediatric infectious disease specialist at Vanderbilt Children's Hospital, just a few days after the adoption was finalized and I'd brought her home to Tennessee.

Since there weren't any detailed records of the medical care she received in Haiti, Dr. Wilson had to establish a baseline for Missy's routine care. He also had to determine a baseline for the Human Immunodeficiency Virus she'd been diagnosed with when she was two and a half—shortly after her birth mom died of AIDS. I knew some of what to expect during Missy's initial hospital visit thanks to the help of a dear friend who had already adopted an HIV+ child from Africa. But I'm not sure anything could've prepared me for that first hour in the waiting room, surrounded by scores of other parents and their seriously ill children. Some were bald because of chemotherapy; some were lying prone on miniature gurneys hooked up to portable ventilators; one was suffering from Proteus Syndrome (the disfiguring disease that Joseph Merrick, also known as the "Elephant Man," suffered from). A few were obviously hanging onto life by a thread.

If you ever find yourself stuck in a prolonged my-life-is-so-hard pity party, I encourage you to spend an afternoon sitting in the waiting room—better yet, handing out balloons—at a children's hospital. You'll be amazed how quickly your own emotional belly button lint becomes boring.

Everything about that inaugural appointment with our infectious disease doc was sobering, but the low point was trying to hold Missy still the first time the phlebotomist drew vial after vial of blood. The many "How to Have a Smooth Adoption Transition" articles I'd devoured emphasized the importance of having someone else hold or immobilize your child while they're being stabbed by healthcare professionals so they don't associate that particular trauma with you, the parent. That sounded so right when I read said articles with bright-eyed and bushy-tailed, soon-to-be-an-adoptive-mama intentions in the safe haven of my local Starbucks. But the reality of that actually happening when you're a single mom and your child has a communicable disease is unlikely.

Plus, I didn't want to delegate the tough stuff to a total stranger since Missy was brand-new to the states, didn't speak English, and was just starting to trust me. The sturdy, chatty, white chick who had seemed nice enough while visiting in Haiti with her suitcase full of suckers had now dragged her into a strange, new world with weird sights, sounds, smells, and *people*.

So after the physical exam, during which she panicked and sobbed and buried her face in my chest even though it wasn't painful or invasive, I picked her up and carried her kicking and screaming down the hall to her first blood draw. Honestly, I would've given just about anything to flee the hospital right then and go someplace else that served hot pancakes instead of big needles. But International House of Pancakes would have to wait because, in that moment, I realized being a good parent doesn't always mean protecting your kids from pain. Sometimes it means allowing them to experience the kind of hurt that leads to healing.

It broke my heart when her face twisted with terror and all thirty-six pounds of her began to tremble violently as the technician moved toward her with the needle. And when she strained against my arms with much more strength than seemed possible for a four-and-a-half-year-old who'd been malnourished most of her life. And when her huge brown eyes burned into mine—first with unbelief, then with indignant fury—as it dawned on her I was complicit with the woman she now refers to as the "mean wady who hort me." I made myself a silent promise then that no matter what, one day I was going to buy my little girl a pony. Or a Porche.

We left the hospital with a list of prescriptions for antiretroviral medicines that will hopefully keep Missy's HIV manageable, and then we ended up going to eleven—yes, *eleven*—different pharmacies trying to fill them. I felt my neck flush hot with anger and frustration after driving all over Middle Tennessee to hear chain-store pharmacist after chain-store pharmacist sheepishly tell me the meds Missy's life depended on, which they'd promised would *definitely* be there, *weren't* there after all. When the very last one shrugged his shoulders with a flimsy excuse, after I'd raced across town to get there before his pharmacy closed, I somehow managed to swallow the unworshipful words that had gathered on the tip of my tongue and turn away from him just as tears began spilling down my cheeks.

I remember shifting Missy from one hip to the other. She'd fallen asleep, completely exhausted after being poked, prodded, weighed, jabbed, and dragged all over Nashville on our elusive meds quest. I felt the sharp protest of tendonitis in my elbow and of the fused discs in my neck and back, none of which were used to toting the dead weight of a floppy, unconscious child, a giant purse, *and* a twenty pound tote filled with new mom "necessities" (one liter of filtered water, antibacterial gel, various snack options, coloring books, crayons, an iPad loaded with kid's games and movies, and the Holy Grail of toddler mothers everywhere, a Costco-sized canister of "Boogie Wipes") for hours at a stretch.

I slowly trudged out of that store thinking, *I've only been this punkin's mom for two days, and I've already failed at the most basic task of getting her prescriptions filled. How in the world am I going to take good care of her if I can't even do this?* Remember that thing I said in the first chapter of this book about the best things in life coming at a high price? Yeah, sometimes I want to kick myself in the shins too.

Missy's illness has caused my health insurance to double, but the financial cost pales next to the emotional premium. I felt like my soul was going to split in two recently when a well-intentioned elderly woman asked Missy if she wanted a Popsicle, then nervously pulled on rubber gloves before handing it to her.

Life is hard, and when you factor in stuff like infectious disease it can be *really* hard. But in true Dickensian fashion, the *worst* aspects of adopting a "high risk" child have led to the *best* chapter of my life. To infinitely more joy, hope, and peace than I could have possibly experienced without her.

A SCENIC POINT ON THE ACTS JOURNEY

At this point in the story of how God's Spirit was moving and empowering the early church, some of its members began emulating the Gospel-bellowing boldness of Peter and fleshing out the declarative promise of Jesus at the beginning of Acts: "But *you will receive power when the Holy Spirit has come upon you*, and *you will be my witnesses* in Jerusalem and in all Judea and Samaria, and to the end of the earth" (Acts 1:8 ESV; emphasis mine). Although, not everyone they witnessed to was receptive:

> Stephen continued speaking: "You stubborn people! You have not given your hearts to God, nor will you listen to him! You are always against what the Holy Spirit is trying to tell you, just as your ancestors were. Your ancestors tried to hurt every prophet who ever lived. Those prophets said long ago that the One who is good would come, but your ancestors killed them. And now you have turned

against and killed the One who is good. You received the law of Moses, which God gave you through his angels, but you haven't obeyed it."

When the leaders heard this, they became furious. They were so mad they were grinding their teeth at Stephen. But Stephen was full of the Holy Spirit. He looked up to heaven and saw the glory of God and Jesus standing at God's right side. He said, "Look! I see heaven open and the Son of Man standing at God's right side."

Then they shouted loudly and covered their ears and all ran at Stephen. They took him out of the city and began to throw stones at him to kill him. And those who told lies against Stephen left their coats with a young man named Saul. While they were throwing stones, Stephen prayed, "Lord Jesus, receive my spirit." He fell on his knees and cried in a loud voice, "Lord, do not hold this sin against them." After Stephen said this, he died.

Saul agreed that the killing of Stephen was good.

On that day the church of Jerusalem began to be persecuted, and all the believers, except the apostles, were scattered throughout Judea and Samaria.

And some religious people buried Stephen and cried loudly for him. Saul was also trying to destroy the church, going from house to house, dragging out men and women and putting them in jail. And wherever they were scattered, they told people the Good News. (Acts 7:51–8:4 NCV)

Stephen, likely a relatively new Christ-follower, was one of seven men the apostles had chosen to manage and allocate charitable giving. There'd been some fussing about how some of the needy folks were getting more financial assistance than others, so they chose a few good men (which many congregations now refer to as *deacons*) to sort it all out (Acts 6:1–4).

Therefore, it stands to reason that Stephen, being a chosen member of the very first deaconate, was a wise, honorable, well-liked kind of guy. He was probably on the school board and raised money for the March of Dimes too. And we know for sure that he was passionate about the gospel because Luke literally describes him as "a man with great faith and full of the Holy Spirit" (Acts 6:5 NCV). So it's not hard to imagine the collective shock and grief that rippled through that neophyte church community when he was stoned to death by a militant, anti-Christian mob simply because of one straightforward sermon about their generational stubborn streak and desperate need for Jesus.

Humanly speaking, it would've made sense for the early church to recoil after the tragedy of their dear friend's gruesome murder and retreat in light of this very "worst of times" event. It'd make sense if they chose to circle their proverbial wagons and focus on consoling the core group of their fellowship. Maybe hire a grief counselor, a crisis manager, and some administrative help to wade through all the insurance and liability issues. But they didn't shrink back in fear. They didn't go underground and become a covert, self-protective, cultish kind of crew. They didn't allow a horrific homicide to curb their cause. Nope. They did the exact opposite. Their commitment to love others for the sake of Christ didn't get buried with Stephen—it rose up and got bigger! The enemy's knock-out punch didn't send them reeling to the canvas; it propelled them to the Witnessing Olympics!

Here's the funny thing about hardship. It tends to have the reverse effect on those who've put their hope in Jesus rather than in their circumstances. Instead of staying down when we're walloped, God's people tend to bounce back with more *oomph*. In fact, church history proves that opposition often works like Miracle-Gro on the body of Christ. The power of the Holy Spirit enables us to have Rocky-like comebacks, pointing to the undefeatable, redemptive power of the gospel. We may be down, but we're never out!

Now back to the story at hand, the day after Stephen's funeral, one of his diaconate buddies named Philip packed an overnight bag, kissed his wife and kids goodbye, and hopped a bus to a place called Samaria to preach the very same message that had incited people to pummel his friend to death with rocks:

> Now those who were scattered went about preaching the word. Philip went down to the city of Samaria and proclaimed to them the Christ. And the crowds with one accord paid attention to what was being said by Philip when they heard him and saw the signs that he did. For

unclean spirits, crying out with a loud voice, came out of many who had them, and many who were paralyzed or lame were healed. So there was much joy in that city. (Acts 8:4–8 ESV)

Phil didn't choose an easy venue to begin his witnessing career. He journeyed to a place that would cause most people of Jewish descent to break out in hives, and all seven men who'd been appointed by the apostles to help administer charitable giving in the early church were Hellenistic Jews—men who were Jewish by birth but conversant in Greek because of where they lived. This was a place where sharing the gospel publicly could get him pelted with rocks, but it was a destination Jesus had already declared His followers would go—to a place called Samaria.

Before we go any further, let's take a minute to camp out on how and why there was such a huge chasm between Jews and Samaritans. How Samaritans were to Jews what a fur coat is to PETA. I mean, these two people groups didn't just march to the beat of a different drum—they were diametrically opposed.

The reason they were is because 750 years before the earthly life and ministry of Jesus Christ, a violent people group called the Assyrians conquered the northern kingdom of Israel where Samaria is located. This resulted in a country where Jews and Assyrians intermarried; typically an Assyrian man took a Jewish wife—among his many other wives—in order to further subjugate the Jews and weaken their bloodlines. They produced a race that was half-Jewish and half-Assyrian, who came to be known as *Samaritans*. For centuries Jewish people vilified Samaritans as impure traitors.

The battle lines deepened over the years. For instance, when the southern Jews returned to Jerusalem after the Babylonian captivity and began to rebuild the temple, the Samaritans offered to help. The Jews said, "No thanks, you bunch of dirty half-breeds." So the Samaritans said, "Fine, you bunch of stuck-up nerds, we'll build our own temple on Mount Gerizim." (I'm obviously taking just a tiny bit of liberty in the nuances of their dialogue, but you get the gist.) Then the Samaritans went on to establish their own priesthood, independent of the Jews, and considered only the first five books of the Torah—the Pentateuch—to be authoritative. The Jews revered the entire compilation of the Law—the historical books, the wisdom books, and the prophets. Essentially, Samaritans disregarded everything Jews held sacred, and Jews fumed to the point of cursing their Samaritan neighbors publicly in the synagogue and praying for Jehovah to exclude them from eternal life.

Which is why this one little passage in Acts 8 is akin to a big dude in black leather roaring down the main aisle of a symphony hall on a Harley past wide-eyed, black-tie-clad concert goers who'd been listening to a formal rendition of Beethoven's *Fifth*. It was jarring in its spiritual significance! The point Luke is making in this Philip-went-to-Samaria narrative (actually *reiterating* since he had already made this point with the story about the Good Samaritan in his Gospel account) is that God's grace is available to *everybody*. Period. His is an unconditional, wholly inclusive affection. There is no skin color, country of origin, or medical condition that can make you incompatible with the love of Jesus Christ!

ARE YOU WILLING TO RISK LOVING MORE PEOPLE, MORE?

Frankly, this next passage in Acts seems to indicate that those whom we prejudice-inclined humans are less likely to accept are the ones most likely to be God's favorites. Because, after Philip witnessed to the Samaritans, he *ran* to share the great news of redemption with a guy even Samaritans would be predisposed to snub:

> An angel of the Lord said to Philip, "Get ready and go south to the road that leads down to Gaza from Jerusalem—the desert road." So Philip got ready and went. On the road he saw a man from Ethiopia, a eunuch. He was an important officer in the service of Candace, the queen of the Ethiopians; he was responsible for taking care of all her money. He had gone to Jerusalem to worship. Now, as he was on his way home, he was sitting in his chariot reading from the book of Isaiah, the prophet. The Spirit said to Philip, "Go to that chariot and stay near it."

So when Philip ran toward the chariot, he heard the man reading from Isaiah the prophet. Philip asked, "Do you understand what you are reading?"

He answered, "How can I understand unless someone explains it to me?" Then he invited Philip to climb in and sit with him. The portion of Scripture he was reading was this:

> *"He was like a sheep being led to be killed.*
> *He was quiet, as a lamb is quiet while its wool is being cut;*
> *he never opened his mouth.*
> *He was shamed and was treated unfairly.*
> *He died without children to continue his family.*
> *His life on earth has ended."*

The officer said to Philip, "Please tell me, who is the prophet talking about—himself or someone else?" Philip began to speak, and starting with this same Scripture, he told the man the Good News about Jesus.

While they were traveling down the road, they came to some water. The officer said, "Look, here is water. What is stopping me from being baptized?" [Philip answered, "If you believe with all your heart, you can." The officer said, "I believe that Jesus Christ is the Son of God."] Then the officer commanded the chariot to stop. Both Philip and the officer went down into the water, and Philip baptized him. When they came up out of the water, the Spirit of the Lord took Philip away; the officer

never saw him again. And the officer continued on his
way home, full of joy. (Acts 8:26–39 NCV)

A couple of the contextual details in this passage just
slay me. First of all, at the very beginning when the angelic
emissary charges Phil to "get ready and go," the meaning
in the original Greek phraseology implies that the order is
to arise and go at midday.[1] To begin his mission trip at high
noon. During the time of day in the Ancient Near East when
it's most likely to be parched-throat hot and thighs-sticking-
to-the-car-seat humid, when everyone else is sprawled on a
couch indoors, enjoying the air conditioning and Diet Coke
and daytime television. It's an *uncomfortable* time to share
the love of Jesus.

Second, the road the shimmering angel dude directs
Philip to take is the Jerusalem-Gaza route, which is basically a side road. A less traveled highway. An *unlikely*,
tumble-weed-strewn kind of place to be sowing divine seed.

And third, the target of Philip's sermon is an Ethiopian
eunuch who, in Jewish religious context, is an "undesirable." Since Luke doesn't go into detail with his description
of this gentleman, scholars aren't sure whether he was a natural eunuch—a male born without complete genitalia—or
whether, as was a typical custom during this time of ancient
history, he'd been surgically deformed as a little boy to ren-
der him sexually harmless in order to be a safe, effective
guardian of a wealthy man's harem. Or perhaps he'd been
given the ceremonial title of eunuch, to distinguish him as

a court official. What *is* clear is that according to Mosaic Law, eunuchs were barred from fully participating in worship (Deuteronomy 23:1).

All those details add up to some rather radical applications regarding evangelism. They suggest that in order to share the love of Jesus Christ we must:

Be willing to feel *uncomfortable*.

Be willing to go to *unlikely* places.

Be willing to connect with *undesirable* people.

WHEN PUSH COMES TO SHOVE AND RISK BECOMES REALITY

Being uncomfortable in unlikely places with "undesirable" people has led to some unbelievable moments of grace in our little corner of the world lately. Like the last time we had Missy's prescriptions filled. Of course, I quickly learned that getting serious meds from the same place where I buy batteries and *People* magazine wasn't the best option, so we found a private pharmacy that specializes in meds for people with HIV and AIDS. They don't sell candy, cards, breakfast cereal, toothpaste, or Chia pets, just pricey medicine for pretty sick folks. It's tucked away on the fifth floor of an old building that used to house a low-budget shopping mall. And if your heart hasn't been calibrated by the Holy Spirit, you might be tempted to judge some of the other customers as less-than-desirable company.

While coming and going or waiting for her scripts to be ready, Missy and I have chatted it up with a few scantily clad ladies of the evening, several rough-looking ex-cons, an HIV+ transvestite in towering red heels, and lots of men in the latter stages of AIDS. The first two groups I'm familiar with because of the time I've spent in addiction recovery groups, but I'd never spent any time around gaunt men with dark circles under their eyes and Kaposi's sarcomas (cancerous dermatological lesions that often accompany late-stage AIDS) marring their skin. That is, until I took a leap of faith and accepted the gift of all things Missy.

Of course, some of these colorful customers gave us a sneaky glance of curiosity too when we first stepped on the elevator with them. This was probably because Missy is usually dressed in her plaid school uniform, black and white saddle shoes, knee socks, and a bow bigger than her head, and I'm usually wrapped in my whole middle-aged, sleep-deprived, harried, white-mama glow. I think they assume we've mistakenly come to the wrong place. Surely a darling mocha-colored kid and her chaperone weren't going to the "special" pharmacy.

Some even hurdle over benign curiosity and jump straight to barely disguised contempt when they first see us. This aptly describes the thin man with cracked lips, multiple sarcomas, and an angry expression whom we rode up the elevator with on our last visit. He literally averted his gaze and exhaled in protest when Missy blurted out happily, "Hello Sur! How awe you?" I put my hand protectively on her shoulder and tried to stealthily scoot her a few inches away from him, but this was one of those times her ardor was not easily redirected. She tugged on his sleeve and persisted with more animation and volume, "I'm Missy Haar-Purr, I'm *five*! And this is my *Mama* Haar-Purr!"

He threw me a look of frustration and exhaled louder, emphasizing his irritation at our presence. It was all I could do not to grin at his look of surprise when we walked into the pharmacy with him and the darling women who run the place swarmed Missy like a bevy of favorite aunts. He seemed startled when they asked her to sing (she has a habit of serenading people she likes), and she responded by belting out the praise chorus of "Your Great Name" followed by an enthusiastic, hip-swiveling encore of "Shake Your Booty." Missy's musical repertoire is surprisingly vast. A few minutes later, after she'd proclaimed, "Happy Tanksgiming" and handed a big sucker to each one of the staff, she turned to him, held up her last remaining lollipop, and asked sweetly, "Wood chu like a sucker, Sur?"

His contempt melted like the wax beneath a lit candle. You could tell by the way his expression softened as he leaned down and replied gently, "Well, yes, honey. I believe I would." My daughter and another mom's very sick son chatted, then she hugged him before bellowing a rather bossy "Happy Tanksgiming, Sur!" and turning to leave. He reached over her head and shook my hand. When our eyes met, we both smiled. I couldn't speak because I was too close to tears. But I don't think we needed any more words. Enough had already been said.

What Thanksgiving does annually for my waistline, Missy has done for my heart. She's increased my capacity for compassion, which is exactly the kind of effect the indwelling power of the Holy Spirit has on Christ-followers. According to Acts, divine grace will cause our hearts to expand far beyond our previous boundaries. The unconditional love God has lavished on us has the ability to level the walls of fear and prejudice that separate us from others. The gospel that compelled Philip to board a Greyhound and preach to marginalized folks in Samaria then strap on Nikes and trot alongside an ostracized man's carriage in order to tell him about the living hope of Jesus Christ is the same gospel that should be compelling us. That means becoming more inclusive and less homogenous as we seek to imitate Christ. It means being brave enough to embrace people we never noticed before. It means loving more people, more.

🔴 Had a great night of worship at Ridgecrest in NC with a wonderful, gracious group of @LifeWay store managers from around the country. Which was basically icing on the cake after getting to see 650+ women run into the arms of Jesus at @womenoffaith. However, I still had a twinge of angst in my spirit as I got ready to speak this afternoon because it's hard to be away from Missy for three days in a row. But then when I got back to my room a few minutes ago this pic popped up on my phone; it's of Missy praying at Legislative Plaza in downtown Nashville tonight for God's will to take place in our nation and the world! She's only five and she's only been in the US for six months, y'all, yet here she is *on her knees praying* in downtown Nashville! Of course, I know some of this may be just her mimicking the adults around her, but she didn't have to. No one made her. So I'm believing that most of what this picture reveals is that my little girl, who doesn't have an earthly daddy, is responding to the loving nature of her heavenly one. He's got her in the palm of His hand! #onlyGod #fathertothefatherless #mistymama

(Instagram post from October 5, 2014)

SIX

Sinners Who Would Be Saints

The very first time I met Missy she called me *Mama*. Of course, I knew she'd been coached by Mike and Missy Wilson, an amazing couple from Nashville who moved to Neply, Haiti, and founded a faith-based residential facility and community outreach program called My Life Speaks to care for unwanted special-needs orphans and others through faith-based programs like a school, worship center, medical clinic, and feeding program. But I didn't care. I was just thrilled she referred to me as "Mama," and I was thrilled that Mike and Missy grinned from ear to ear and nodded with approval when I took her in my arms for the first time.

The Wilsons' endorsement was a big deal because they'd loved Missy like one of their own since she was an infant. Several times a week her Grandmom or Great Aunt FiFi brought her to visit them at the My Life Speaks community center for a hot meal. Oftentimes those simple meals served on Monday, Wednesday, and Friday were all my baby had to eat during the week. Like most people in her village, her caregivers were extremely impoverished and had no outside help. Many of the kids in Neply suffer from mild to severe malnourishment. But Mike and Missy didn't just give my Missy physical nourishment, they also held her and played with her and sang songs to her. She was just one of the hundreds of barefoot, hungry, miniature image-bearers they felt called to help care for, but she happened to be an especially winsome one. It wasn't unusual for her to get an extra serving of rice and beans or a little more lap-sitting time!

However, when Missy was two-and-a-half years old a villager raced into the mission courtyard and breathlessly asked if someone from My Life Speaks could drive Missy's mom to the hospital in Port-au-Prince. (Very few people in Neply own or even have access to a vehicle.) That's when the Wilsons met Marie, my daughter's birth mother. Only a few hours later, after jostling wildly for several hours over deeply rutted roads from their rural outpost to the hospital in Haiti's bustling capitol city of more than a million people, a doctor approached them and gravely explained that Marie had died of AIDS. Like most Haitians, she'd never been tested and didn't know she had the disease. He soberly asked if the toddler Missy Wilson was holding on her lap was Marie's biological child.

Big Missy told me her heart sank to her stomach as she answered, "Yes, this is Marie's youngest child," all the while silently praying, "Please God, not this one. Please don't let her be any sicker than she already is." Unfortunately, her blood tests soon confirmed that little Missy had HIV. Not long afterward, Haitian authorities informed Mike and Missy that My Life Speaks's operating license didn't allow them to house a child with HIV, so they needed to place her in a government-sanctioned orphanage for children with infectious diseases (where she would likely die within months without sufficient care or medicine) or find someone willing to formally adopt her so that their adoption fees could pay for the medical treatment she so desperately needed.

In the perfect sovereignty of God, an old friend of mine named Michelle Smalling was visiting the Wilsons the week Marie passed away. She'd made the harried, heartbreaking trip to the hospital with them. She was there when they got the bad news about little Missy. And she listened when the Holy Spirit whispered to her immediately afterward, "Lisa Harper is supposed to be her new mom." So Michelle told them she knew a woman in Nashville who'd just lost a domestic adoption. She explained that since I was single, I was trying to adopt a child who didn't have much of a chance. She said if they were open to the idea, she'd call me as soon as she returned to the States to see if I was willing to become Missy's mama.

Six weeks later I landed at the Port-au-Prince airport, and several gut-churning hours in an old diesel, fume-spewing school bus after that, I walked into the My Life Speaks community center and was handed a nineteen-pound little girl who regarded me with serious, somewhat suspicious brown eyes, then grabbed my pinkie with a surprisingly strong grip and croaked a greeting with the moniker I instantly loved more than any other name I've ever been called, "Halo, *Mama Blanc*."

You'd think that after two whole years and five lengthy visits with her in Haiti during which she called me *Mama* the entire time, Missy would continue calling me *Mama* when I brought her home to Tennessee. But no sooner had we landed at the Nashville airport to a raucous welcome home party than she began referring to me as *Pablo*. Occasionally she called me *Mama Blanc* (which means "white mama" or "non-Haitian mama"), but more often than not she referred to me as *Pablo*.

It didn't bother me at first. I figured she was going through such an enormous transition she'd simply forgotten my name. *Poor little punkin' is being bombarded with so many new words, she's overwhelmed. It'll come back to her soon enough. Plus, it could be a lot worse,* I reasoned. *She could be calling me "pale, chunky stranger who talks a lot" or something. At least it's a name. Heck, it's way better than "Hey You" or "Crazy-Kidnapper-Chick."*

But when my new title persisted for a month, I begin to wonder if Missy would ever call me *Mama* again. I imagined going to school functions and smiling awkwardly when other parents said, "Oh you must be Missy's mom, *Pablo*." Or grimacing inwardly when she introduced me to her first date as, "This is the lady I live with, *Pablo*." Or sighing inappropriately when the pastor turned to me at her wedding and asked, "Do you, *Pablo*, give your daughter's hand in marriage to this man?" It's not that I have any problem with the name Pablo—I think it's a lovely name for Hispanic men—it's just not one I readily identified with. And I couldn't figure out why she'd seized on it.

It wasn't until I talked with a physician who was familiar with Missy's orphanage that the mystery of Pablo was resolved. About a year into the adoption process, we had to move Missy from Neply to Dr. Jacob Bernard's orphanage, New Life Link, in Peytonville, Haiti, for legal and medical reasons. There were several vacation Bible school lessons on the missionary journeys of Paul soon after Missy arrived at New Life Link. In an attempt to give her a better understanding of who I was, one of the nannies at the orphanage told Missy I traveled around America talking to people about Jesus . . . kind of like a *missionary*. Missy put two and two together and decided that Paul (called "Pablo" by her teachers) and I were one and the same.

I laughed out loud when we figured out the genesis of *Pablo* because I could totally picture that incomparable preacher, missionary, church-planter, and avid letter-writer rolling his eyes in glory and complaining to God about how he'd prefer a more sanctified, manly doppelganger! But I was also flattered by Missy's extremely generous assumption. I still think *Mama* is the best word in the human vocabulary, which thankfully she resumed calling me after a month or so of Pablo/Paul. But being confused with the saint who penned thirteen of the twenty-seven books in the New Testament ranks really high up on my sweet and undeserved gifts list!

A SCENIC POINT ON THE ACTS JOURNEY

I do feel obliged to clarify that Paul's brief autobiography in Philippians reveals that, in all likelihood, we are *not* related:

> For we are the circumcision, who worship by the Spirit of God and glory in Christ Jesus and put no confidence in the flesh—though I myself have reason for confidence in the flesh also. If anyone else thinks he has reason for confidence in the flesh, I have more: circumcised on the eighth day, of the people of Israel, of the tribe of Benjamin, a Hebrew of Hebrews; as to the law, a Pharisee; as to zeal, a persecutor of the church; as to righteousness under the law, blameless. (Philippians 3:3–6 ESV)

The man Missy confused me with went by the name "Saul" before changing to "Paul" in Acts 13. He was born into a wealthy Jewish family in a city called Tarsus, which is now located in the country of Turkey. His parents had the honorable distinction of being Roman citizens, which was atypical for Jews and usually meant they'd made some kind of significant contribution to the Roman Empire. Therefore Paul's family essentially lived in a gated community, drove European cars with heated leather seats, got ushered to the best seats at the best restaurants in town, *and* were smiled at with approval when they passed by. They got invited to all the elite, black-tie fundraisers in Tarsus and wrote the biggest checks in return. They had affluence and admiration. Power and position.

So, of course, Paul was educated at the best private schools and was sent to Jerusalem around the age of fourteen to apprentice under a wise and prominent Rabbi (Hebrew for "teacher") named Gamaliel. The very same guy who sagely counseled the high priest of Israel and a posse of Jewish leaders not to kill Peter and the apostles in Acts 5:17–42 but to just wait and see how the new religious movement they were leading played out.

> Followers of Jesus Christ weren't called Christians until the second half of the first century in the Syrian capital of Antioch (Acts 11:26). Scholars believe the term was coined by anti-Christian leaders who intended it to be derogatory.

Anyway, Paul's star had risen high in Jewish social circles at the same time the early church was experiencing explosive growth. He was considered to be one of Gamaliel's most promising protégés because of his excellent pedigree, his exceptional intelligence, and his exceedingly strong will. However, unlike his mentor, Paul didn't favor a wait-and-see approach with regard to Jesus' disciples and the message of grace they were preaching. As a militant defender of Judaism, he was fiercely opposed to their belief system, which was initially labeled "The Way" (Acts 9:2).[1] Given the dangerous potential it had to divert fellow Jews away from Judaism (all of the first converts in Acts were Jews), Paul went to great lengths to quash it, including sending, in effect, a congratulatory group text to the mob that murdered Stephen:

> They took him out of the city and began to throw stones at him to kill him. And those who told lies against Stephen left their coats with a young man named Saul. While they were throwing stones, Stephen prayed, "Lord Jesus, receive my spirit." He fell on his knees and cried in a loud voice, "Lord, do not hold this sin against them." After Stephen said this, he died.
> Saul agreed that the killing of Stephen was good. (Acts 7:58–8:1 NCV)

And squiring another goon squad around in his Mercedes from one neighborhood to another on a "seek and destroy all Christians" mission: "Saul was also trying to destroy the church, going from house to house, dragging out men and women and putting them in jail" (Acts 8:3 NCV).

But while driving to Damascus on yet another anti-Christian operation, Saul/Paul ran into an impassable roadblock:

> Meanwhile, Saul was uttering threats with every breath and was eager to kill the Lord's followers. So he went to the high priest. He requested letters addressed to the

synagogues in Damascus, asking for their cooperation in the arrest of any followers of the Way he found there. He wanted to bring them—both men and women—back to Jerusalem in chains.

As he was approaching Damascus on this mission, a light from heaven suddenly shone down around him. He fell to the ground and heard a voice saying to him, "Saul! Saul! Why are you persecuting me?"

"Who are you, lord?" Saul asked.

And the voice replied, "I am Jesus, the one you are persecuting! Now get up and go into the city, and you will be told what you must do."

The men with Saul stood speechless, for they heard the sound of someone's voice but saw no one! Saul picked himself up off the ground, but when he opened his eyes he was blind. So his companions led him by the hand to Damascus. He remained there blind for three days and did not eat or drink. (Acts 9:1–9 NLT)

Suffice it to say, Paul's collision with the Messiah he'd ridiculed and whom he'd persecuted others for believing in had blinding, heart-searing, life-changing consequences. For three days he holed up in a friend's condo and replayed his conversation with the King of all kings over and over again in his head. Then, after a complete stranger paid him a visit that corresponded exactly with his God-given dream, the lights came on and Paul realized he had no choice but to repent and follow Jesus:

There was a follower of Jesus in Damascus named Ananias. The Lord spoke to Ananias in a vision, "Ananias!"

Ananias answered, "Here I am, Lord."

The Lord said to him, "Get up and go to Straight Street. Find the house of Judas, and ask for a man named Saul from the city of Tarsus. He is there now, praying. Saul has seen a vision in which a man named Ananias comes to him and lays his hands on him. Then he is able to see again."

But Ananias answered, "Lord, many people have told me about this man and the terrible things he did to your holy people in Jerusalem. Now he has come here to Damascus, and the leading priests have given him the power to arrest everyone who worships you."

But the Lord said to Ananias, "Go! I have chosen Saul for an important work. He must tell about me to those who are not Jews, to kings, and to the people of Israel. I will show him how much he must suffer for my name."

So Ananias went to the house of Judas. He laid his hands on Saul and said, "Brother Saul, the Lord Jesus sent me. He is the one you saw on the road on your way here. He sent me so that you can see again and be filled with the Holy Spirit." Immediately, something that looked like fish scales fell from Saul's eyes, and he was able to see again! Then Saul got up and was baptized. After he ate some food, his strength returned.

Saul stayed with the followers of Jesus in Damascus for a few days. Soon he began to preach about Jesus in the synagogues, saying, "Jesus is the Son of God."

All the people who heard him were amazed. They said, "This is the man who was in Jerusalem trying to destroy those who trust in this name! He came here to arrest the followers of Jesus and take them back to the leading priests."

But Saul grew more powerful. His proofs that Jesus is the Christ were so strong that his own people in Damascus could not argue with him. (Acts 9:10–22 NCV)

I don't think anyone would disagree with the fact that Paul had a radical conversion. And that led to a radical commitment, which theologian and eminent Pauline scholar F. F. Bruce describes like this:

"With astonishing suddenness the persecutor of the church became the apostle of Jesus Christ. He was in mid-course as a zealot for the law, bent on checking a plague which threatened the life of Israel, when, in his own words, he was 'apprehended by Christ Jesus' (Philippians 3:12) and constrained to turn right round and become a champion of the cause which, up to that moment, he had been endeavouring to exterminate, dedicated henceforth to building up what he had been doing his best to demolish."[2]

Paul's abrupt reversal led to him being chased out of Damascus by his former colleagues for preaching the Good News of Jesus Christ, so he headed back to Jerusalem on a mission completely the opposite of the take-all-Christians-captive one he charged out of there on earlier (Acts 9:26). He hustled home to witness to his old schoolmates and family members in Tarsus (Acts 9:30), and after receiving a private Facebook message from Barnabas talking about a possible revival brewing in Antioch, he threw a duffel bag in the trunk of his now-dusty, high-mileage Mercedes on yet another mission trip (Acts 11:25–26). Not to mention that all of this traveling-to-tell-people-about-Jesus took place before his three "officially sanctioned" missionary journeys recorded in Acts 13, 16, and 19, and it doesn't include his three-year preaching stint in Arabia (Galatians 1:17–18)!

> Paul's letters—the primary source of our knowledge about the beginning of Christianity and the template for much Christian doctrine and theology—are also the earliest datable Christian documents, written between eighteen and thirty years after the death and resurrection of Jesus Christ.[3]

However, Paul's radical commitment to preach the grace-based gospel message of:

Faith in Jesus + Nothing = Salvation

to people all over the civilized first-century world came at a radical cost, which he enumerates in his second letter to a church he founded in Corinth:

> Five times the Jews have given me their punishment of thirty-nine lashes with a whip. Three different times I was beaten with rods. One time I was almost stoned to death. Three times I was in ships that wrecked, and one of those times I spent a night and a day in the sea. I have gone on many travels and have been in danger from rivers, thieves, my own people, the Jews, and those who are not Jews. I have been in danger in cities, in places where no one lives, and on the sea. And I have been in danger with false Christians. I have done hard and tiring work, and many times I did not sleep. I have been hungry and thirsty, and many times I have been without food. I have been cold and without clothes. Besides all this, there is on me every day the load of my concern for all the churches. I feel weak every time someone is weak, and I feel upset every time someone is led into sin. (2 Corinthians 11:24–29 NCV)

Ultimately, the dramatic change the Apostle Paul experienced on the road to Damascus cost him his life. According to historical documents, this would-be-saint was most likely beheaded around AD 68 on the outskirts of Rome, the city he was once so proud to be called a citizen of.

Paul always had the Latin name *Paullus* (Greek, παῦλος) because he was born a Roman citizen (Acts 22:28). Every Roman citizen had three names or *tria nomina*, consisting of a *praenómen* (forename), *nómen* (family name), and *cognómen* (personal name). Most scholars believe that Paul is the apostle's *cognomen*. His *praenomen* and *nomen* are unknown.

Paul also had another name, a signum or supernomen—Saul, his Hebrew name.[4] Therefore some scholars believe that when "Saul" began going by the name "Paul" during his first sanctioned missionary journey to Cyprus (Acts 13), he was simply switching to a moniker that the mostly Gentile world he felt called to preach in would be more comfortable with.

ARE YOU WILLING TO RISK CHANGING YOUR COURSE?

My dad, Everett Andrew Harper, experienced his own version of a Damascus Road encounter with Jesus Christ while he was walking the perimeter of his property in a rural part of Central Florida in 1979. Being the owner of forty-two sandy acres that were dotted with scrub oaks and grazed by fifty bored-looking Holsteins may not sound quite as impressive as being a wealthy, well-educated Roman citizen like Paul, but owning that modest ranch meant the world to my dad. Mostly because when he was a little boy his dad lost their family farm in the wake of the Great Depression. As a result, their family moved from a comfortable life in Tennessee to a hardscrabble one in West Palm Beach, Florida, where my paternal grandfather took the only job he could find managing a commercial dairy farm.

So Dad spent the remainder of his youth getting up at four o'clock in the morning—rain or shine—to help his father milk several hundred cows. Then he'd grab a boiled egg for breakfast, kiss his mama goodbye, and walk several miles to school in shoes with holes in the soles. When the dismissal bang rang, he'd hustle home, grab a pail, and join his daddy in the barn to begin the laborious multi-hour milking process all over again. He told me that during the long, hard years of adolescence when he felt like a grubby thorn among elegant roses (West Palm Beach is one of the wealthiest cities per capita in the US), he vowed to make a lot of money when he grew up so *his* family would never suffer from material want. That desire to reclaim the life his father lost drove my dad down a destructive path for much of his adult life.

He worshipped Jesus publicly on Sunday and most Wednesday nights too, but during the rest of the week he worshipped at the altar of financial success. He pushed himself and those around him hard in a mission to create a small empire that included an insurance firm and a residential and commercial building and development company. He wasn't opposed to cutting a few corners or getting his hands a little dirty in the process, either. Dad's hard-nosed style led to marginal business triumphs in his thirties and forties and enough money to buy his beloved ranch and drive new-model trucks around town. But after a development deal went horribly wrong when I was in high school, he was forced to file bankruptcy and lost everything he owned.

The night before the bank foreclosed on the ranch, he couldn't sleep. So he began walking around the property, grieving his misfortune. Grieving the fact that he was in midlife—past the energy and earning potential of his youth—and facing the same humiliating ruin that befell his father. And that's when the Spirit of the Living God dropped my daddy to his knees. Right there on a two-lane dirt road between the Holstein pasture and the Texas Longhorn bull enclosure, Jesus knocked the wind out of his prideful sails. He later told me that it's the first and only time he saw a bright light that he believed to be of divine origin.

Dad Harper changed his course dramatically after that night. He said God was giving him a second chance to do life right. Instead of being motivated by money, he was going to try to honor Jesus with whatever he had. Now single—my stepmother, dad's third wife, fell in love with the veterinarian at the beginning of his financial downturn and left before he went bankrupt—Dad moved into a little one-bedroom apartment and began spending his free time volunteering at a homeless shelter and teaching Bible studies at the Orlando County Jail. The final three decades of Dad's story were wholly different from the first five.

One of the last coherent requests he made in the days leading up to his death was for us to change him into his "good" pajamas and slippers. My mom, who had reconciled with Dad during the last year of his life and became his dear friend, my sister, and I demurred because we were afraid that jostling him in his frail condition would cause too much pain. But he was gruffly insistent. I finally explained our reticence and said, "Daddy, the pajamas you're wearing right now are fine. They're clean, I promise." He fixed his blue eyes on mine and croaked firmly, "Lisa, I'm about to be dancing on streets of gold, and I don't want to go up there in old pajamas and bare feet."

More people than we could count came up to us at his funeral not only to express their condolences but also to express that knowing Dad had changed the course of their lives. They told us his passion for Jesus had ignited theirs. That his generosity had inspired them to give more away. That his determination to love others for the sake of Christ was the way they hoped to live. When Dad died, there wasn't much money in his estate, but he left my sister and me with an immeasurably valuable legacy of faith.

WHEN PUSH COMES TO SHOVE AND RISK BECOMES REALITY

Some of my best Thanksgiving memories include Dad and me driving to a sketchy part of Orlando in his old truck and serving dinner to homeless people at the faith-based mission run by his friend. My rough-around-the-edges yet tenderhearted father instilled in me an affinity for people who are walking through difficult seasons. Dad's love for the "downtrodden"—a term he used based on his lifelong preference for the King James Version of the Bible—is one of the main reasons I started volunteering at The Next Door.

Not too long ago, I was explaining to a new group of residents who had gathered for a small Bible study I lead there that the hour we got to spend together was sacred and safe. The only rule was that they had to respect each other and themselves. I went on to assure them they didn't have to pretend that they believed in Jesus if they didn't. I would much rather they be honest about their faith or lack thereof. However, if they genuinely engaged with the true stories about His life, death, resurrection, and perfect love for people, I was convinced they'd end up falling in love with Him. When I finished my spiel, a surly looking woman wearing a camouflage flak jacket, who'd been staring at the floor with her arms crossed and a defiant look on her face the whole time, glanced up.

She hesitated for a second or two—obviously unsure about my whole "you can be honest in here" speech—then verbalized her jaded unbelief in a rush, "I think all this Jesus stuff is bull—, and I think you're a big bull—er. The only reason I'm in here is 'cause graduating from this shi—y program is one of the conditions for my parole, and coming to this stupid Bible study is one of the dumba—conditions of this stupid program." Before I could help myself, I burst out laughing. Fiery personalities like hers usually tickled Dad, and I could picture him chuckling.

The tension in the room quickly dissipated when the giggle virus infected every member of our motley little crew, including the doubter. A month or so later that precious girl put her faith in the unconditional love of Jesus Christ and eventually graduated from the program, landed a decent job, and had her children returned from social services after proving she could be a loving, responsible parent. She made a remarkable change of course during the six months she lived at The Next Door, although she affectionately insisted on referring to me as "The B—S'er" the whole time—a name I came to appreciate almost as much as Pablo!

Before Missy, I assumed motherhood was all about balance. But I'm learning it has more to do with discernment—recognizing which proverbial balls to juggle, which to drop, and when to sing silly songs on the way to school even though she clogged her toilet yet again this morning and I have a wad of almond butter stuck in my hair. #ilovethislife #olddogscanlearnnewtricks

(Instagram post from November 5, 2014)

SEVEN

A Compassionate Compulsion

I went on my first mission trip in December 1970 when I was seven years old. However, I didn't go to Jerusalem or Judea or Samaria. Instead, I pulled a red wagon full of green mistletoe bundles tied with red rubber bands to the end of Valencia Street, about eleven houses down from the one I grew up in. It took me at least an hour to get to the end of the block because I stopped at every single house along the way, knocked on the door, and asked if they wanted to buy Christmas mistletoe for the low, low price of a quarter per bunch. My goal was to make twelve dollars hawking the hang-it-up-and-force-people-to-kiss weed I'd climbed a huge oak tree to harvest, so that I could buy Mom a gold-plated necklace from J. C. Penney for Christmas. She was completely unaware of my door-to-door beggarly campaign and surely would've stopped me had she known what I was up to.

Sales were brisk until I banged on the Greenburg's door, which was opened almost immediately by a smiling Mrs.

Greenburg. She said, "Well, hello, Lisa, and what do you have here?" gesturing to the wagon. "Hi, Mrs. Greenburg," I said with a grin, which I'm sure widened when I launched into my holiday spiel, "I'm selling special Christmas mistletoe for only a quarter a bunch, would you like to buy some?" She replied kindly but firmly, "Honey, we don't celebrate Christmas because we're Jewish."

It was the first time I'd ever met *anybody* who didn't celebrate Christmas, which I found quite troubling. So when she invited me inside for a glass of Kool-Aid, I proceeded to share a play-by-play version of the birth, life, death, and resurrection of Jesus as best I could remember from our lengthy flannel board lessons in Southern Baptist Sunday school. The details of my first evangelistic visit are still clear to this day because Mrs. Greenburg called Mom that afternoon, spilled the beans on my secret mistletoe campaign, and recounted our conversation with good humor. Then she arranged a time for me to come back to their house for a playdate with her daughter.

A year after what some might call a mistletastrophe, Esther Greenburg and I were sitting on one of the highest branches of the old magnolia tree in our front yard when she confided that her father was moving them back to Israel even though she and her mom didn't want to leave America. After promising each other we'd be best friends forever, we held hands and prayed. Because by then Esther had decided that the Jesus I couldn't not jabber about must be the real deal and had secretly asked Him to come into her heart too.

A SCENIC POINT ON THE ACTS JOURNEY

I know the phrase "couldn't not" is a grammatically incorrect double negative, but I think it effectively describes the determination early Christians had when it came to sharing the glorious hope of the gospel. The exuberant zeal with which they were fulfilling the second declarative promise of Jesus from Acts 1—"you will be my witnesses in Jerusalem and in all Judea and Samaria, and to the end of the earth" (Acts 1:8 ESV)—had a brave, confrontational, shot-out-of-a-cannon feel to it in spite of the fact that their first official mission trip took place after Stephen's murder and Peter's escape from prison:

> In the church at Antioch there were these prophets and teachers: Barnabas, Simeon (also called Niger), Lucius (from the city of Cyrene), Manaen (who had grown up with Herod, the ruler), and Saul. They were all worshiping the Lord and fasting for a certain time. During this time the Holy Spirit said to them, "Set apart for me Barnabas and Saul to do a special work for which I have chosen them."
>
> So after they fasted and prayed, they laid their hands on Barnabas and Saul and sent them out.
>
> Barnabas and Saul, sent out by the Holy Spirit, went to the city of Seleucia. From there they sailed to the island of Cyprus. When they came to Salamis, they preached the Good News of God in the synagogues. John Mark was with them to help.

They went across the whole island to Paphos where they met a magician named Bar-Jesus. He was a false prophet who always stayed close to Sergius Paulus, the governor and a smart man. He asked Barnabas and Saul to come to him, because he wanted to hear the message of God. But Elymas, the magician, was against them. (Elymas is the name for Bar-Jesus in the Greek language.) He tried to stop the governor from believing in Jesus. But Saul, who was also called Paul, was filled with the Holy Spirit. He looked straight at Elymas and said, "You son of the devil! You are an enemy of everything that is right! You are full of evil tricks and lies, always trying to change the Lord's truths into lies. Now the Lord will touch you, and you will be blind. For a time you will not be able to see anything—not even the light from the sun."

Then everything became dark for Elymas, and he walked around, trying to find someone to lead him by the hand. When the governor saw this, he believed because he was amazed at the teaching about the Lord. (Acts 13:1–12 NCV)

The fact that Paul chose to temporarily blind Elymas, the evil magician, tickles me. I suppose since that's how God stopped him in his destructive, pre-conversion tracks, he decided it'd be an effective tool to use on other anti-Christian folks too! And Paul's zapping detractors method obviously worked this time. Much like my childhood friend, Esther, the governor of this coastal city on the southwest side of

Cyprus was so undone by the message Paul and Barnabas shared about Jesus Christ that he put his trust in the Lord.

More often than not, though, the direct missionary style of the early Christians was woven with tangible respect and compassion for whomever they were attempting to evangelize. For instance, consider the content and context of Paul's sermon to a group of presumably stuffy Jewish leaders at the end of that first mission trip:

> Paul and those with him sailed from Paphos and came to Perga, in Pamphylia. There John Mark left them to return to Jerusalem. They continued their trip from Perga and went to Antioch, a city in Pisidia. On the Sabbath day they went into the synagogue and sat down. After the law of Moses and the writings of the prophets were read, the leaders of the synagogue sent a message to Paul and Barnabas: "Brothers, if you have any message that will encourage the people, please speak."
>
> Paul stood up, raised his hand, and said, "You Israelites and you who worship God, please listen! The God of the Israelites chose our ancestors. He made the people great during the time they lived in Egypt, and he brought them out of that country with great power. And he was patient with them for forty years in the desert. God destroyed seven nations in the land of Canaan and gave the land to his people. All this happened in about four hundred fifty years.
>
> "After this, God gave them judges until the time of

Samuel the prophet. Then the people asked for a king, so God gave them Saul son of Kish. Saul was from the tribe of Benjamin and was king for forty years. After God took him away, God made David their king. God said about him: 'I have found in David son of Jesse the kind of man I want. He will do all I want him to do.' So God has brought Jesus, one of David's descendants, to Israel to be its Savior, as he promised. Before Jesus came, John preached to all the people of Israel about a baptism of changed hearts and lives. When he was finishing his work, he said, 'Who do you think I am? I am not the Christ. He is coming later, and I am not worthy to untie his sandals.'

"Brothers, sons of the family of Abraham, and others who worship God, listen! The news about this salvation has been sent to us. Those who live in Jerusalem and their leaders did not realize that Jesus was the Savior. They did not understand the words that the prophets wrote, which are read every Sabbath day. But they made them come true when they said Jesus was guilty. They could not find any real reason for Jesus to be put to death, but they asked Pilate to have him killed. When they had done to him all that the Scriptures had said, they took him down from the cross and laid him in a tomb. But God raised him up from the dead! After this, for many days, those who had gone with Jesus from Galilee to Jerusalem saw him. They are now his witnesses to the people. We tell you the Good News about the promise God made to our ancestors. God has made this promise come true for us, his children, by raising Jesus from the dead. We read about this also in Psalm 2:

'You are my Son.
Today I have become your Father.'

God raised Jesus from the dead, and he will never go back to the grave and become dust. So God said:

'I will give you the holy and sure blessings
that I promised to David.'

But in another place God says:

'You will not let your Holy One rot.'

David did God's will during his lifetime. Then he died and was buried beside his ancestors, and his body did rot in the grave. But the One God raised from the dead did not rot in the grave. Brothers, understand what we are telling you: You can have forgiveness of your sins through Jesus. The law of Moses could not free you from your sins. But through Jesus everyone who believes is free from all sins. Be careful! Don't let what the prophets said happen to you:

'Listen, you people who doubt!
You can wonder, and then die.

> *I will do something in your lifetime*
> *that you won't believe even when you are told*
> *about it!'"*

While Paul and Barnabas were leaving the synagogue, the people asked them to tell them more about
these things on the next Sabbath. When the meeting was
over, many people with those who had changed to worship God followed Paul and Barnabas from that place.
Paul and Barnabas were persuading them to continue
trusting in God's grace. (Acts 13:13–43 NCV)

I know that's a hefty chunk of Scripture, but even if
you just choose to skim it, you'll see that long before Paul
brings up the subject of Jesus, he establishes a connection
with his Torah-trained audience by reciting Jewish history
and several Old Testament Torah passages. In other words,
he doesn't come prancing in with gospel guns blazing and
shoot up what's sacred to them. Instead, he finds genuine
common ground and builds his case from there. He doesn't
treat these Israelite men like a conversion project—he relates
to them like would-be friends. And that respectful, relational style is evident again during a conversation Paul has
with some much-more-liberated Greek intellectuals during
the third official mission trip of Acts:

While Paul was waiting for them in Athens, he was
greatly distressed to see that the city was full of idols.

So he reasoned in the synagogue with both Jews and God-fearing Greeks, as well as in the marketplace day by day with those who happened to be there. A group of Epicurean and Stoic philosophers began to debate with him. Some of them asked, "What is this babbler trying to say?" Others remarked, "He seems to be advocating foreign gods." They said this because Paul was preaching the good news about Jesus and the resurrection. Then they took him and brought him to a meeting of the Areopagus, where they said to him, "May we know what this new teaching is that you are presenting? You are bringing some strange ideas to our ears, and we would like to know what they mean." (All the Athenians and the foreigners who lived there spent their time doing nothing but talking about and listening to the latest ideas.)

Paul then stood up in the meeting of the Areopagus and said: *"People of Athens! I see that in every way you are very religious. For as I walked around and looked carefully at your objects of worship, I even found an altar with this inscription: to an unknown god. So you are ignorant of the very thing you worship—and this is what I am going to proclaim to you.*

"The God who made the world and everything in it is the Lord of heaven and earth and does not live in temples built by human hands. And he is not served by human hands, as if he needed anything. Rather, he himself gives everyone life and breath and everything else. From one man he made all the nations, that they should inhabit the whole earth; and he marked out their appointed times in history and the boundaries of their lands. God did this so that they would seek him and perhaps reach out for him and find him, though he is not far from any one of us. *'For in him we live and move and have our being.'* As some of your own poets have said, 'We are his offspring.'

"Therefore since we are God's offspring, we should not think that the divine being is like gold or silver or stone—an image made by human design and skill. In the past God overlooked such ignorance, but now he commands all people everywhere to repent. For he has set a day when he will judge the world with justice by the man he has appointed. He has given proof of this to everyone by raising him from the dead."

When they heard about the resurrection of the dead, some of them sneered, but others said, "We want to hear you again on this subject." At that, Paul left the Council. Some of the people became followers of Paul and believed. Among them was Dionysius, a member of the Areopagus, also a woman named Damaris, and a number of others. (Acts 17:16–34 NIV, emphasis mine)

In his opening remarks to this Grecian group, Paul compliments them on their attention to religion. He observes the fact that they've erected idols and altars all over town out of deference to the pantheon (the entire collection of Greek gods and goddesses; "pantheon" is also the name of the ancient Roman temple dedicated to those same gods and goddesses) and how they'd gone so far as to consecrate one to an anonymous "god" just to make sure their bases were covered! Then Paul says, "For in him we live and move and have our being" in his argument for the veracity of the gospel. I've heard that recited for as long as I can remember, but it wasn't until we studied the book of Acts in seminary that I found out it didn't originate with Scripture. Instead it was written by a Greek poet in lyrics that were dedicated to Zeus, who was considered the "father of gods and men"—essentially the big daddy of the pantheon in Greek mythology.

The bottom line is the early missionaries didn't try to coerce people from other cultures to look, think, and act like them; instead, they found creative ways to connect with them so they could *share* the message of redemption. Their God-given compulsion to witness was riddled with love and respect.

ARE YOU WILLING TO RISK GOING SOMEWHERE TO WITNESS TO SOMEONE?

As wonderful as my first mistletoe-hawking that morphed into a mission trip turned out to be, I ended up convinced I wasn't actually wired for evangelism. Because that first sweet brush with evangelism when I was a kid was followed by multiple evangelistic train-wrecks over the next fifteen years. One happened when our youth group leader forced us to go door to door in a run-down apartment complex and I ended up disturbing an angry man in an awkward state of undress. He jerked me into his living room and gave me an intense scolding for interrupting his nap. Making matters much worse, the whole time he was swinging his arms and fuming about the appalling gall of high school kids nowadays, his robe kept gaping open to reveal way more than I needed to see. To this day, I feel anxious around large, gesturing men.

Then there was the time in college that a particularly self-righteous camp counselor condemned me for being reluctant to approach a family I'd never met before in a state park. He'd typed out a fake survey and attached it to an official-looking clipboard so I could "gain people's trust and then surprise them with a sneak gospel attack."

Finally there was the time I was encouraged to book a seat separate from other youth ministry colleagues while flying to my first national staff conference in order to ask a total stranger the two classic Evangelism Explosion questions:

1. Have you reached the point in your spiritual life where you know for certain that if you were to die tonight you would go to heaven?
2. If you were to die tonight and God were to ask you, "Why should I let you into heaven," how would you answer?

I truly respect the ministry of EE and the positive impact it continues to have in training Christians around the world how to more effectively share their faith. However, I think those "diagnostic" questions work best when asked in the context of some kind of relationship. Because when an immature twenty-two-year-old woman turns to a fifty-something-year-old businessman—who's minding his own business and reading the *Wall Street Journal*—in the very confined setting of adjoining airplane seats and chirps those questions, things are likely to go awry. The businessman may even assume the perky missionary has insider information about the safety of the aluminum tube they're currently cruising in at thirty-five thousand feet.

When our flight finally landed in Atlanta—much to my seatmate's relief—my boss corralled the rest of us in the gate area so we could dialogue about what happened during our mile-high missions opportunity. He went on to explain that everyone needed to disclose our individual conversations verbatim for "accountability" purposes. As soon as I finished relating mine, it was apparent that I was by far the weakest link on the team. My coworkers looked down and feigned sudden interest in the airport carpeting out of sympathy over my incompetence. But my boss looked me directly in the eyes for a few seconds. Then he shook his head sadly and muttered, "I guess you just don't have the gift of evangelism." At which point I hung my head and completely agreed with him.

After that I decided I would try to become the nicest Christian I could possibly be but would never again sully the cause of Christ by trying to witness to unbelievers. I reasoned, *I'll love my neighbor like Jesus says, but I'm not gonna "share my faith" verbally unless somebody asks me a direct question about it.* That way, I figured no one would get hurt. Neither myself nor some poor pagan who happened to wander into my vicinity.

The fault with my former furlough rationale is that it's impossible to carve the witnessing element out of the commandment Jesus gave us to love others: "You shall love the Lord your God with all your heart and with all your soul and with all your strength and with all your mind, and your neighbor as yourself" (Luke 10:27 ESV). It's also impossible to consciously ignore the commissioning part of His farewell address: "Go therefore and make disciples of all nations, baptizing them in the name of the Father and of the Son and of the Holy Spirit, teaching them to observe all that I have commanded you. And behold, I am with you always, to the end of the age" (Matthew 28:19–20 ESV). And there isn't a convenient personality or preference clause in His second declarative promise of Acts either. Jesus *didn't* say: "You will be my witnesses in Jerusalem and in all Judea and Samaria, and to the end of the earth *if* you're a willing, well-spoken extrovert armed with a proven evangelism strategy."

The bottom line is that going somewhere to tell someone about the good news of Jesus is a common calling for believers. Being sent by the Holy Spirit for the purpose of sharing our faith is a universal sacrament, not a selective "gift." If we've put our trust in the life, death, and resurrection of Jesus Christ, we don't have the option of bowing out of the "whole evangelism thing" as a reticent friend of mine says. To be a Christian is to be compelled to share the message that saved us. Peter said it well: "Always be prepared to give an answer to everyone who asks you to give the reason for the hope that you have" (1 Peter 3:15 NIV). And I love the metaphor late hymn writer D. T. Niles wraps around our communal calling: "Evangelism is just one beggar telling another beggar where to find bread!"[1]

WHEN PUSH COMES TO SHOVE AND RISK BECOMES REALITY

I've spent most of my adult life in vocational ministry. I've had the privilege of telling stories about the unconditional love of Jesus Christ at retreats and conferences around the country, writing books and Bible studies about Him, and have even been given the opportunity to share the living hope of the gospel in many countries across Africa, Europe, and North and Central America. But by far the most difficult place I've ever had the privilege of sharing my faith was in my own home with my stepfather, John Angel.

He and mom got married when I was six years old. It was a year after my parent's divorce was finalized and not long after I'd been sexually molested by a couple of men who posed as family "friends" during the dark season following Dad Harper's departure. To say I was desperate for a safe father figure is putting it mildly. At first John seemed to fit the bill. He was a superintendent of schools in Central Florida, so he was good with kids and well respected in our community. He was also quick to laugh and head over heels in love with Mom. It wasn't until after their honeymoon, when he moved into our house, that Dad Angel's disdain for anything that had to do with Jesus emerged.

Sometimes his disdain was relatively mild, like when he acquiesced to Mom's insistence about praying at mealtimes but exhaled or sighed loudly throughout even the briefest of invocations. But sometimes his disdain took a nasty turn, like when he hurled my Bible out the front door with an expletive because he "didn't want that book of lies in his house" anymore. The only time I can remember him saying the word "God" was when it was followed by the word "damn." And when I was in my early twenties and told him I'd decided to leave the field of marketing and take a job with a youth ministry, he declared that mine was going to be the worst waste of a mind he'd ever seen. Soon afterward, I wrote a paraphrase of Saint Augustine's famous confession in the front of my Bible: "Lord, may my heart not find perfect rest in thee until Dad Angel's does."

I must've shared the gospel with him a hundred times. I was compelled to insert the topic of Jesus into our conversations, often in stilted religious responses to his articulate

Darwinian logic or with way too much emotionalism for an extremely masculine, lifelong academic to handle. If we'd had the technology of texting back then, I would've showered him with emoticons. Thank goodness God spared him that one. Dad Angel and I discussed our divergent beliefs about sin and redemption for over twenty years. But then I gave up. I didn't make a deliberate decision to quit or anything; I just stopped praying for him on a daily basis. Then I stopped looking for opportunities to engage him in dialogue about God. Eventually I stopped telling him stories about the miracles I'd seen—stories of hard-core crack addicts who'd gotten clean because of the restorative grace of Jesus, kids who'd quit cutting themselves because of His unconditional love, and couples who'd reconciled because of the healing power of His forgiveness.

As my hope for his salvation faded, I slowly withdrew my heart from him too. I did my subconscious best to stop caring. Seven years later—a jubilee's worth of time—Dad Angel put his hope in Jesus after my eleven-year-old nephew, John Michael, shared the gospel with him for the bazillionth time. Two months later I had the undeserved honor of leading his graveside service because, as he explained to Mom, "I want Lisa to do it because I don't like any of the other preachers I know."

Here's what the Holy Spirit whispered to me over and over again in those two months leading up to his death: *I didn't need you to save your dad. I just want you to love him.* I've taught similar lessons to audiences around the world, but I didn't walk it with Dad Angel until the twilight of his life. That's when I really understood that witnessing to unbelievers isn't so much about the message that falls out of our mouths; it's more about the posture of our hearts. Because a gospel that's not compelled by compassion isn't very good news at all.

> Because we loved you so much, we were delighted to share with you not only the gospel of God but our lives as well. (1 Thessalonians 2:8 NIV)

The first thing Missy asked during her inaugural Santa visit was, "Do you know Jebus?" (The poor guy glanced at me quizzically, and I had to explain how I'd told her that he's one of Jesus' friends here on earth who helps with all the birthday festivities and whatnot because they didn't have Santa in her part of Haiti and she was initially quite confused by all the chunky-dude-in-red-velvet hubbub.) I still find myself smiling about her innocent boldness with Mr. Claus and can't help thinking that hers is really the essential question of the season. Do you know Jebus/Jesus? Jesus, the divine Hero who condescended to be clothed in flesh and born in a barn that very first Christmas. Jesus, who lived a perfect, sinless life so that His sacrificial death that very first Easter would have the power to reconcile mankind with our Creator. Jesus, the only One who's willing to lavish every single mistake-prone one of us with perfect, unconditional compassion that will never fade or fail. Do you know *this* Jesus? If not, I hope you have enough courage—or maybe even enough desperation—to be like the wise men and seek Him. Because if you do, you'll find Him. And then you'll actually get to live a life saturated with the love, joy, hope, and peace everybody's singing about this time of year.

(Instagram post from December 15, 2012)

EIGHT

The Need to Be Regospeled

Because Missy's birth parents were Haitian, she and I don't look *exactly* alike. We do have very similar smiles—except I currently have a few more teeth up front than her—matching brown eyes, and lots of identical mannerisms. We share the habit of shouting, "Yes!" and raising our arms in a victory salute when presented with a favorite snack, and we both untuck the sheets at the end of the bed before going to sleep because otherwise our feet feel trapped. People who've known me all my life say they can't imagine a daughter more suited for me. However, her hair is a lot curlier than mine and some people have a problem with that.

Because I live in the southeastern United States, where folks who have very strong opinions about hair texture tend to congregate, I tried to prepare myself for the inevitable prejudice we could expect before bringing Missy home. I read multiple books on the subject, had long, frank discussions with a few close friends who have really curly hair, watched several documentaries, and sought the wisdom of a professional adoption transition specialist.

So the first few sideways glances and insensitive comments we received didn't faze me much. It was actually pretty easy to shrug them off and muse: *they don't know what they're missing,* especially since Missy was oblivious to the slights. But the first time Missy was a direct recipient of bigotry was a whole other matter. It happened in the children's play area of the Southwest Airlines concourse in the Nashville airport. I noticed the culprit and her kids out of the corner of my eye before they even staged their mini-playground takeover. Let me rephrase that. I think everybody within one hundred feet noticed her because she was shrieking into a cell phone at full, extra-twangy, grammatically challenged volume. And she was wearing an extremely revealing outfit.

I'm not a prude, y'all. I mean, I'm for modesty and all, but I'm so not one of those uptight Bible-thumper ladies who advocates for long denim skirts and turtlenecks or anything. I grew up in Central Florida near the beach and worked as a lifeguard every summer in high school and college, so for years I thought pants were optional! But this chick in the airport transgressed every modicum of public appearance unless you live in a nudist colony. Honestly, a bandana would've provided more coverage. And based on the way she was alternating between yelling at whoever was on the other end of the phone and hollering at her three angry-looking offspring, her parenting skills were as meager as her choice of attire.

The bottom line is, my mama bear radar was up before my cub got attacked. But I still wasn't prepared for the white hot anger that exploded in my gut when trashy-mama's much older daughter shoved mine at the top of the slide, put her sassy little hands on her hips, waggled her finger accusingly in Missy's stunned face, and spat out with scorn, "You are b-l-a-c-k, BLACK!" Her mean-spirited taunt echoed through the gate area and caused several businessmen to glance up from their *USA Today*s with eyebrows arched in surprise. Then several heads swiveled in my direction, including the little stinker who'd just threatened my angel.

Time seemed to stand still for a moment, and I felt the blood rush to my head in a classic fight-or-flight response. I was suddenly acutely aware of the sound of my own heartbeat and that of air being exhaled loudly through my nostrils like a bull about to charge. The next few seconds seemed to unfold in slow motion as I fixed my narrow-eyed glare on the now-slack-jawed juvenile offender standing before me in a too-small dress her mother had obviously picked out. After a very long pause during which she visibly cowered, I pointed at her menacingly and mouthed these words slowly and with great exaggeration: *I'm . . . going . . . to . . . cut . . . you.*

Okay, the whole story's true until that last part. I didn't really mouth *I'm going to cut you* to a nine year old. And the person I actually wanted to mouth it to was her mother, who was, of course, still bellowing into the phone and had missed the entire drama. Because bullies aren't born, they're made.

My guess is that poor little girl's mama or daddy or

grandmom or granddad or aunt or uncle or Sunday school teacher had gone to great lengths to narrow her young mind and inject her fragile heart with prejudiced poison. Some cretin had *taught* her that certain people groups were less valuable than others based on the shade of their skin, or their country of origin, or the texture of their hair, or maybe even the lack of spandex in their clothes. They handed an innocent child a weapon of mass destruction, a hierarchy by which to legitimize hatred. Sadly, it wouldn't surprise me if the perpetrator of that hogwash was a religious person, because we have a history of denying others the very same grace that saved our sorry selves.

A SCENIC POINT ON THE ACTS JOURNEY

So far we've covered how our spiritual ancestors were exhibiting true community through generosity, joy, and devotion; how they were experiencing exponential growth in spite of fierce opposition and physical violence; how they were witnessing the dramatic conversion and transformation of former foes like Paul; and how they were responding to the gospel with missional zeal. In short, the early church was a lean, mean fighting machine. They were cooking with gas. They were cruising at full speed. They were in high cotton. With the exception of a few bad apples like Ananias and Sapphira, the book of Acts depicts them as being a vibrant, cohesive, efficacious crew of Christ followers. That is until the devastating bully of bigotry threatened to trample their cause:

> Then some people came to Antioch from Judea and began teaching the non-Jewish believers: "You cannot be saved if you are not circumcised as Moses taught us." Paul and Barnabas were against this teaching and argued with them about it. So the church decided to send Paul, Barnabas, and some others to Jerusalem where they could talk more about this with the apostles and elders.
>
> The church helped them leave on the trip, and they went through the countries of Phoenicia and Samaria, telling all about how the other nations had turned to God. This made all the believers very happy. When they arrived in Jerusalem, they were welcomed by the apostles, the elders, and the church. Paul, Barnabas, and the others told about everything God had done with them. But some of the believers who belonged to the Pharisee group came forward and said, "The non-Jewish believers must be circumcised. They must be told to obey the law of Moses."
>
> The apostles and the elders gathered to consider this problem. (Acts 15:1–6 NCV)

In other words, some of the Jewish converts to Christianity decided Gentile converts weren't "good enough" to be accepted into God's family unless they looked and acted like Jews. Just like the little girl in the airport who snubbed Missy, or the elderly man who glared at us and muttered, "That's disgusting," when Missy and I walked past him holding hands on Main Street in downtown Franklin recently, the Judean Bible teachers were sewing divisive seeds of prejudice in the Antioch church plant.

We've already established that Satan, the enemy of our soul whose passion is to rob, steal, kill, and destroy, is savvy enough to make toxins taste good so we'll swallow them. In this case, he played on the long history of these immature Jewish converts. From the time they were in utero they'd heard Torah at home, in their neighborhood synagogues, and at the temple during major Jewish festivals like Pentecost. Before they could begin to wrap their minds around the meaning of these 613 moral and ceremonial laws that comprise the core of Judaism, they could recite most of them. And they'd spent the better part of every waking moment trying not to break one.

The vast majority of occurrences of the word *torah* in the Bible refer to God's instructions to Moses at Sinai that were later transmitted to Israel. These instructions or commandments (in a narrower or wider sense) became Israelite law and the stipulations of the old covenant.

Adding weight to an already crushing burden, the Jewish priesthood came up with an interpretation of Torah called the Talmud, which is basically the first application-oriented Bible study. All 613 rules came with a detailed instruction manual. Therefore, in order to maintain good standing in the community, religious Jews had to be meticulous about every single facet of life, including but not limited to: worship, fashion, grooming, vocations, vacations, physical ailments, mental ailments, sexual intimacy, and what they could or could not eat. Their adherence to minutia shaped unique behavioral patterns and appearances, like long coiled sideburns on men, hair coverings on women, gasps of horror if they got too close to anything bloody, and a strong aversion to bacon cheeseburgers.

Needless to say, Jewish individuals who converted to Christianity in the book of Acts were initially such scrupulous rule-followers they'd make a modern-day, non-drinking, non-smoking, non-dancing Baptist look like a prodigal on steroids! So it's no wonder they were having a hard time with the fraternity-brother-ish Gentile converts who'd seemingly sailed in from a laissez-faire, lawless background and hadn't "earned" the grace of God they were now reveling in. Which is why the Jewish Christians decided to erect a hierarchical ladder with a few more steps leading to redemption. They adapted the "Faith in Jesus + Nothing = Salvation" message Peter, Stephen, and Paul had preached to be a "Faith in Jesus + A Restrictive Menu and Circumcision = Salvation" lecture. They surmised it was a harmless enough edit; *I mean, we aren't expecting non-Jews to adhere to all 613 Torah rules or anything, just the biggies. All they have to do is order their steaks medium well and agree to get their private parts tweaked a bit. Plus, that's just a teensy outpatient surgery, and they'll only be sore for a day or two afterward. Heck, we'll even pay for the icepacks.*

This prejudiced-based friction that endangered the fellowship of the early church is officially titled "The Jerusalem Debate," and it caused such a rift in Antioch that Paul and Barnabas traveled back to Jerusalem to try to sort the matter out with the rest of the elders and apostles. It's easy to imagine the murmurs of differing opinions that were rippling through the multi-ethnic congregation of our mother church when Peter stood up to address them:

> After a long debate, Peter stood up and said to them, "Brothers, you know that in the early days God chose me from among you to preach the Good News to the nations. They heard the Good News from me, and they believed. God, who knows the thoughts of everyone, accepted them. He showed this to us by giving them the Holy Spirit, just as he did to us. To God, those people are not different from us. When they believed, he made their hearts pure. So now why are you testing God by putting a heavy load around the necks of the non-Jewish believers? It is a load that neither we nor our ancestors were able to carry. But we believe that we and they too will be saved by the grace of the Lord Jesus." (Acts 15:7–11 NCV)

The first point Peter argues is that the gospel they'd been preaching:

Faith in Jesus + Nothing = Salvation

had already resulted in an international harvest of salvations. So obviously the Holy Spirit was able to soften sinners' hearts unto repentance without first whacking them over the head with a fifty-pound rule book. The testimony of Jesus Christ crucified and resurrected was perfectly sufficient to compel the lost to find their living hope in Him. The melody of *solo fide* (Latin terminology for "faith alone," which is how the early church explained that the justification for human sin happens through faith, not through works and/ or behavioral modification) didn't need the accompaniment of external conformity. God's mercy was able to pierce— ahem, *circumcise*—people's hearts without anybody having to pull their pants down.

While the audience was still digesting that logic, he pulled the rug out from underneath them with this point: "So it makes no sense to me that some of you are testing God by burdening His disciples with a load that neither our forefathers nor we have been able to carry" (Acts 15:10 THE VOICE).

Yep. That includes you, Curly-Kosher boy.

I bet most of the men listening to Pete argue his case were now acutely aware of the sound of their own heartbeats and air being exhaled loudly through their nostrils.

Surely some of them were slack-jawed with the realization that he'd just nailed them to the wall with his observation: *the weight of the law almost broke your backs, so why in the heck are you so determined to strap it on someone else's shoulders?*

Here's the deal about the judgment God declared as a result of humanity's sin against Him (Psalm 110; Joel 3:12; Romans 3:23): We. Can. Never. Behave. Well. Enough. To. Satisfy. It. We can't *get* good enough. No matter how many biblical rules we're able to keep, how many items we can check off a religious list, how many levels we ascend on some man-made tier, it's impossible for humans to attain perfection. And perfection is the only remedy for God's wrath. So, He had to send His only begotten Son into the world wrapped in a suit of skin to live a *perfect* sinless life, shed His *perfect* blood during a sacrificial death, which made *perfect* atonement for our sin. Jesus was the only One who could justify us and reconcile us into a right relationship with our heavenly Father. If we could close the gap with God ourselves, Jesus could've just kept chilling out in glory and skipped the whole sordid "Redeeming Mankind" mission.

The Mosaic Law these well-intentioned Jewish Christians in Acts were so fired up about getting Gentiles to abide by *never* had the power to save anyone. That wasn't God's intention when He gave it to Moses in the first place. God didn't proclaim those commandments on that ancient pinnacle so that by them we could be saved, but so that by them we'd realize we can't save ourselves! The Old Testament moral and ceremonial stipulations underscore our absolute inability to achieve perfection. They were always, always, always meant to lead us to Jesus.

Which confirms Peter's argument. Divine grace has to be free because none of us could possibly afford it. Furthermore, our *gratitude* for God's grace—not the attempt to justify it—must be the motive behind Christian morality. Otherwise, "good behavior" and "good doctrine" will soon distort into dreadful excuses for condescension, self-righteousness, oppression, bigotry, and even genocide. Simply Google "Hitler" or "Hutus and Tutsis" if you want more current historical examples of the devastation caused by a perverted human understanding of what "good" is.

ARE YOU WILLING TO RISK YOUR PREFERENCES FOR OTHER PEOPLE'S SPIRITUAL BENEFIT?

Paul and Barnabas agreed that they should book a flight back to Antioch with a letter stamped by the mother church clarifying that *anyone* who put his or her faith in Jesus was completely saved by God's grace:

> There was dead silence. No one said a word. With the room quiet, Barnabas and Paul reported matter-of-factly on the miracles and wonders God had done among the other nations through their ministry. The silence deepened; you could hear a pin drop.

James broke the silence. "Friends, listen. Simeon has told us the story of how God at the very outset made sure that racial outsiders were included. This is in perfect agreement with the words of the prophets:

> *After this, I'm coming back;*
> *I'll rebuild David's ruined house;*
> *I'll put all the pieces together again;*
> *I'll make it look like new*
> *So outsiders who seek will find,*
> *so they'll have a place to come to,*
> *All the pagan peoples*
> *included in what I'm doing.*

"God said it and now he's doing it. It's no afterthought; he's always known he would do this.

"So here is my decision: We're not going to unnecessarily burden non-Jewish people who turn to the Master. We'll write them a letter and tell them, 'Be careful to not get involved in activities connected with idols, to guard the morality of sex and marriage, to not serve food offensive to Jewish Christians—blood, for instance.' This is basic wisdom from Moses, preached and honored for centuries now in city after city as we have met and kept the Sabbath."

Everyone agreed: apostles, leaders, all the people. They picked Judas (nicknamed Barsabbas) and Silas—they both carried considerable weight in the church—and sent them to Antioch with Paul and Barnabas with this letter:

From the apostles and leaders, your friends,
to our friends in Antioch, Syria, and Cilicia:

Hello!

We heard that some men from our church went to you and said things that confused and upset you. Mind you, they had no authority from us; we didn't send them. We have agreed unanimously to pick representatives and send them to you with our good friends Barnabas and Paul. We picked men we knew you could trust, Judas and Silas—they've looked death in the face time and again for the sake of our Master Jesus Christ. We've sent them to confirm in a face-to-face meeting with you what we've written.

It seemed to the Holy Spirit and to us that you should not be saddled with any crushing burden, but be responsible only for these bare necessities: Be careful not to get involved in activities connected with idols; avoid serving food offensive to Jewish Christians (blood, for instance); and guard the morality of sex and marriage.

These guidelines are sufficient to keep relations congenial between us. And God be with you!

And so off they went to Antioch. On arrival, they gathered the church and read the letter. The people were greatly relieved and pleased. Judas and Silas, good preachers both of them, strengthened their new friends with many words of courage and hope. Then it was time to go home. They were sent off by their new friends with laughter and embraces all around to report back to those who had sent them. (Acts 15:12–34 THE MESSAGE)

I'd love to tell you that the matter of our being saved by God's grace was settled then once and for all, but if I did, I'd be fibbing. Of course you already know that because, like me, I'm sure you've have a hard time hanging onto the concept for yourself. Divine grace is a truism that's more slippery than wet soap. So it probably won't surprise you that this exact same issue, which threatened to divide the church in Acts, reared its ugly head again in a Galatian church plant soon thereafter. However, it might give you pause to find out this time the rule-following ringleader is Peter:

When Peter came to Antioch, I challenged him to his face, because he was wrong. Peter ate with the non-Jewish people until some Jewish people sent from James came to Antioch. When they arrived, Peter stopped eating with those who weren't Jewish, and he separated himself from them. He was afraid of the Jews. So Peter was a hypocrite, as were the other Jewish believers who joined with him. Even Barnabas was influenced by what these Jewish believers did. When I saw they were not following the truth of the Good News, I spoke to Peter in front of them all. I said, "Peter, you are a Jew, but you are not living like a Jew. You are living like those who are not Jewish. So why do you now try to force those who are not Jewish to live like Jews?"

We were not born as non-Jewish "sinners," but as Jews. Yet we know that a person is made right with God not by following the law, but by trusting in Jesus Christ. So we, too, have put our faith in Christ Jesus, that we might be made right with God because we trusted in Christ. It is not because we followed the law, because no one can be made right with God by following the law.

We Jews came to Christ, trying to be made right with God, and it became clear that we are sinners, too. Does this mean that Christ encourages sin? No! But I would really be wrong to begin teaching again those things that I gave up. It was the law that put me to death, and I died to the law so that I can now live for God. I was put to death on the cross with Christ, and I do not live any-more—it is Christ who lives in me. I still live in my body, but I live by faith in the Son of God who loved me and gave himself to save me. By saying these things I am not going against God's grace. Just the opposite, if the law could make us right with God, then Christ's death would be useless. (Galatians 2:11–21 NCV)

Paul's admonition of Peter for being pharisaical so soon after the Jerusalem Debate, where Pete preached on that very topic, illustrates the word one of my favorite podcast preachers, Matt Chandler from The Village Church in Texas, has coined: *regospeled*. Chandler asserts that Christians need to be "regospeled" on a regular basis because we are so quick to drift from the true gospel of

Faith in Jesus + Nothing = Salvation

It's in our spiritual genes. Before the ink was dry on our mother church's vision statement, our Christian forefathers were prone to preach grace but live by a

Faith in Jesus + My Religious Preferences = Salvation

perversion and impose that impure hogwash on whomever they bumped up against.

WHEN PUSH COMES TO SHOVE AND RISK BECOMES REALITY

Violet Liuzzo is the only white woman honored at the Civil Rights Memorial in Montgomery, Alabama. She was a thirty-nine-year-old housewife and mother of five from Detroit. She was bright, inquisitive, and energetic, but like most suburban housewives she probably wouldn't be remembered as remarkable by anyone other than her family if not for the events of March 25, 1965.

On that remarkable spring day, more than twenty-five thousand demonstrators marched into downtown Montgomery, finishing a five-day, fifty-four-mile trek that began in Selma. Led by Dr. Martin Luther King Jr., these men, women, and children marched to protest the corrupt voter registration system of Alabama, wherein most black Americans were denied the right to cast a ballot.

When the throng finally made it to the steps of the State Capitol Building, Dr. King delivered these lines as part of his rousing "How Long" address:

> The end we seek, is a society at peace with itself, a society that can live with its conscience. . . . I know you are asking today, 'How long will it take?' . . . I come to say to you this afternoon, however difficult the moment, however frustrating the hour, it will not be long, because truth crushed to the earth will rise again.[1]

Sadly, not long after Dr. King concluded his speech, Violet Liuzzo was murdered by Ku Klux Klan members for ferrying marchers back to Selma in her Oldsmobile.

Four good ol' boys pulled alongside her at a red light and shot her twice in the face because they were furious that a Caucasian woman would lend the use of her car, much less extend her hand of friendship, to young men and women with skin the same lovely shade of brown as my daughter's.

President Lyndon B. Johnson eulogized her the next night on national television saying, "Mrs. Liuzzo went to Alabama to serve the struggle for justice. She was murdered by the enemies of justice who for decades have used the rope and the gun, the tar and the feathers to terrorize their neighbors."[2]

Unfortunately, prejudice and bigotry are like kudzu vines; they're hard to get rid of. Several months later, during Mrs. Liuzzo's murder trial, the blatantly racist defense attorney referred to Violet as "a white n—," a disparagement I refuse to dignify by typing it out. The overriding message of his hate-filled rhetoric was that Violet Liuzzo's homicide was justified because of the company she kept. In his miniscule mind, she had absolutely no business fraternizing with really curly-headed people. He thought the only folks pale people should befriend were other pale ones.

The first time I read Violet Liuzzo's story, I wept over the unjust cruelty of her death and millions of others like her who've been abused or murdered as the result of senseless bigotry, fearmongering, and ethnic "cleansing." I came across it a second time in the wake of the devastating conflict that's swept America recently after several tragic altercations between young, unarmed African American men and police officers. And I found myself crying again.

Then I was compelled to get on my knees and pray. Not so much because I can identify with Mrs. Liuzzo or young black men, but because I *can't* identify with those who hate other people simply because of the hue of their skin. Buried somewhere very deep in my crooked sinner-saved-by-grace heart is the toxic belief that I'm somehow more worthy of God's love than that racist defense attorney in Alabama or the scantily clad mother of the first child to bully mine.

To really believe the gospel means I have to be willing to lay down my prejudices too. God help me that there's even a wisp of assumption flitting through my mind that I'm somehow less offensive than a world-class bigot. Sign me up: I need to be regospeled *today*!

The folks at this 103-year-old gas station and deli in the boondocks of TN called my baby "honey," asked for hugs, and made her turkey sandwich extra thick. Thankfully, very few Southerners are prejudiced stinkers like those portrayed on TV!

(Instagram post from July 1, 2014)

NINE

Bearing the Chain Because

Some people can be downright snarky. One chick questioned my parenting skills on Instagram because I posted a picture of Missy in the airport, and in her opinion five-year-olds shouldn't fly as often as my daughter does. Of course, I've never met this particular detractor, so she can't begin to know the genuine worship and Christian community Missy gets to experience while watching new friends in new places run full tilt toward Jesus. She's never heard Missy giggle when the plane takes off and then squeal, "I lub this, Mama!" She's not privy to our itinerary, so she's unaware that I take Missy to less than half of the conferences and events where I have the privilege of teaching, but when she comes along my little girl gets to swim in hotel pools, visit children's museums, and explore unique places around our amazing United States of America. Nor is this woman my professional adoption transition counselor who advised me to spend as much time with Missy as possible—especially during this first year—regardless of whether that means being on the road together, at home relaxing, or singing in the car to and from school so as to cement our relationship as mother and daughter. She couldn't possibly know the ongoing questions that plague single mothers like: "Do I leave her with a babysitter or take her to Texas with me?" as we do our very best to guide and nurture children without the benefit of a daddy with skin on. Nope, that woman hurled a brick at our glass house without the context of any real knowledge of how our lives work or any relationship with us whatsoever, so her criticism seems unfair.

However, her dig at my motherhood shortcomings pales next to the barbs I've received about my shortcomings as a Bible teacher. Mostly due to my informal teaching style and the tendency to weave pop culture into biblical narrative or to refer to the Apostle Peter as "Pete," several online critics have branded me a heretic. One complained that I'm a narcissistic windbag who "never sheds any true light on Scripture." Another qualified her negative review with the fact that her husband and I attended the same seminary, so she bought my book assuming I'd have sound theology. She was deeply disappointed by the casual way I dealt with the Holy Writ and questioned how he and I could've come from the same academic background. And of course there was the woman whose chief complaint was that I was too chubby to be an effective video-based Bible teacher! Again, in light of the fact that I've never met any of these critics or had the opportunity to engage in conversation with them, their criticism seems unfair.

But the seemingly unfair criticism I've endured is child's play compared to the vehement attacks most of my heroes of the faith have withstood. Beth Moore, one of the most humble, seeking-Jesus-on-her-knees saints I've ever met, is regularly branded a dangerous heretic and a false prophet by an organized, mean-spirited gang. These hate-mongers comb through her written or recorded material from books, conferences, Bible studies, blogs, and church services, then splice and dice her words in an ever crueler effort to discredit her. The vitriol Beth and other gospel carriers at her level of visibility bravely tolerate on a regular basis is blatantly unfair. However, it sure doesn't appear to weaken their resolve to run hard after God! Pastor Brian Houston of Hillsong Church in Sydney, Australia, demonstrated this recently when he proclaimed, "No mature Christian who is seasoned in the Word has any reasonable excuse to live their life offended." He went on to explain that, although we will all *be* offended, we don't have to *live* offended.

A SCENIC POINT ON THE ACTS JOURNEY

The last few chapters of Acts illustrate that the injustice of those early Christ-followers' persecution didn't dampen their fiery passion to preach the gospel. In fact, the unfairness of the burdens they bore actually helped prove the worthiness of their cause:

One day as we were going down to the place of prayer, we met a slave girl who had a spirit that enabled her to tell the future. She earned a lot of money for her masters by telling fortunes. She followed Paul and the rest of us, shouting, "These men are servants of the Most High God, and they have come to tell you how to be saved."

This went on day after day until Paul got so exasperated that he turned and said to the demon within her, "I command you in the name of Jesus Christ to come out of her." And instantly it left her.

Her masters' hopes of wealth were now shattered, so they grabbed Paul and Silas and dragged them before the authorities at the marketplace. "The whole city is in an uproar because of these Jews!" they shouted to the city officials. "They are teaching customs that are illegal for us Romans to practice."

A mob quickly formed against Paul and Silas, and the city officials ordered them stripped and beaten with wooden rods. They were severely beaten, and then they were thrown into prison. The jailer was ordered to make sure they didn't escape. So the jailer put them into the inner dungeon and clamped their feet in the stocks. (Acts 16:16–24 NLT)

The New Living Translation clarifies the gist of this passage: a slave girl, whose demonic knack for fortune-telling had been manipulated by her masters for financial gain, got healed as a result of tagging along behind Paul and Silas.

And when the human vending machine got unplugged and the revenue she provided dried up, her unscrupulous owners got really ticked at the missionaries who pulled the plug and demanded they be held accountable for their disruption of Exploitation Inc. So the city officials, who'd likely received bribes from Exploitation Inc. or were concerned that the message Paul and Silas were preaching might disrupt their self-centered practices too, ordered the dynamic preaching duo to be stripped, savagely beaten, shackled, and thrown into a dungeon.

In more formal translations of Scripture, this adolescent clairvoyant is described as "having a pythonic spirit" or being a "pythoness," which means she was inspired by Apollo, the Greek deity associated with the giving of oracles. Therefore, her involuntary utterances were considered to be authoritative "words from god," although not from the one true Trinitarian God Paul and Silas were preaching about, but a member of the Pantheon, the collection of lowercase-g gods and goddesses touted in Greek mythology.[1] Funny how the little-g god vexing the heart and mind of this poor girl prompted her to amble along behind Paul and Silas and babble about the legitimacy of their capital-G God. It reminds me of the verse in James: "You believe that God is one; you do well. Even the demons believe—and shudder!" (James 2:19 ESV).

The fact that Paul and Silas were persecuted and bound for untying this young woman's cords of supernatural mental torment and natural human oppression is entirely unfair. They should've been given a medal and a parade for being heroes in the war against human trafficking. Instead, they're savagely attacked and shoved into solitary confinement with their legs clamped apart in heavy stocks, which added painful cramping to the indignity of being stripped, bruised, and bloodied.

Yet according to Luke, they didn't utter one single word of protest. They didn't yell, "Hang on a minute, you bunch of hotheads, we were just helping that poor girl! Her owners are horrible people who forced her into fortune-telling here in Philippi just to fatten their own bank accounts! Ask her. She's a victim and so are we! Check the facts, y'all. At the very least, please give us a court-appointed attorney so we can prove our innocence!" Instead they submitted to wholly unjust torture. They demonstrated once more that they were "full of joy because they were given the honor of suffering disgrace for Jesus" (Acts 5:41 NCV).

They were honored to be dishonored for the sake of the gospel.

Good night, that's tough to swallow. I mean, I can understand the whole "forgiving seventy times seven" command Jesus gave Pete in Matthew's Gospel:

Then Peter came to Jesus and asked, "Lord, when my fellow believer sins against me, how many times must I forgive him? Should I forgive him as many as seven times?" Jesus answered, "I tell you, you must forgive him more than seven times. You must forgive him even if he wrongs you seventy times seven. (Matthew 18:21–22 NCV)

But I tend to conveniently forget He expects us to be *joyful* in the forgiving process.

The only way I can possibly forgive my trespassers without at least a teensy bit of resentment is to remember the end game. To remember that much like the tournament championship the Karate Kid ultimately won by surrendering to that dreadful "wax on, wax off" routine, there's an amazing reward at the end of suffering for Christ's sake too. Based on Paul and Silas's silent compliance with their undeserved whipping and incarceration, followed by the loud, celebratory worship service they had at midnight *in jail* (they had to be singing with gusto for the other prisoners to hear them) which we'll read about next, I can't help but wonder if the Holy Spirit had already given them a glimpse of the giant spiritual trophy they would ultimately receive:

Around midnight Paul and Silas were praying and singing hymns to God, and the other prisoners were listening. Suddenly, there was a massive earthquake, and the prison was shaken to its foundations. All the doors immediately flew open, and the chains of every prisoner fell off! The jailer woke up to see the prison doors wide open. He assumed the prisoners had escaped, so he drew his sword to kill himself. But Paul shouted to him, "Stop! Don't kill yourself! We are all here!"

The jailer called for lights and ran to the dungeon and fell down trembling before Paul and Silas. Then he brought them out and asked, "Sirs, what must I do to be saved?"

They replied, "Believe in the Lord Jesus and you will be saved, along with everyone in your household." And they shared the word of the Lord with him and with all who lived in his household. Even at that hour of the night, the jailer cared for them and washed their wounds. Then he and everyone in his household were immediately baptized. He brought them into his house and set a meal before them, and he and his entire household rejoiced because they all believed in God. (Acts 16:25–34 NLT)

Before jumping to the obvious miracle of their jailor's conversion, I simply have to linger on the phrase "the prisoners were listening" for a second because there's a miracle encased in it as well. The Greek verb used in this phrase—*epakroaomai*—is an imperfect indicative verb, which is a fancy way of saying the other inmates listened *continually* to Paul and Silas, and they were listening with intense joyfulness. These rough and tumble prisoners were eagerly hearing and responding to a musical gospel message![2] Plus, since Paul convinced the jailor not to commit an "honorable" suicide by proclaiming that no one had escaped—that every single prisoner had remained in their cells in spite of the wide-open penitentiary doors—it implies his new orange-coverall-clad buddies with meaty, tattooed biceps probably became believers as well!

And don't you know those convicts cheered themselves hoarse when the prison superintendent, the same dude who'd ordered Paul and Silas's brutal treatment the day before, bowed respectfully before them and sincerely asked what *he* needed to do to be saved! Early church father, Saint John Chrysostom (AD 349–407), poignantly describes what happens next, "He washed and was washed, he washed them from their stripes, and was himself washed from his sins."[3]

My high school chemistry teacher, Judy Bales, taught me that something has to be burned for combustion to happen, and I think the same concept is often true with the gospel. When believers remain radically faithful during painfully singed seasons, it tends to breed revival. Maybe because just as heat brings impurities to the surface and reveals the rich luster of precious metal, so fiery trials can verify the sincerity of an evangelist. God sometimes allows what is not fair to befall His beloved so the cosmic story of redemption can be confirmed in us and through us.

Adversity and unfair opposition follow the apostles throughout the rest of Luke's narrative in Acts, including two more lengthy incarcerations for Paul. First, when his fellow Jews went all postal and attacked him after assuming he'd brought a Gentile into the temple and desecrated it:

When the seven days of their purification were nearly up, some Jews from around Ephesus spotted him in the Temple. At once they turned the place upside-down. They grabbed Paul and started yelling at the top of their lungs, "Help! You Israelites, help! This is the man who is going all over the world telling lies against us and our religion and this place. He's even brought Greeks in here and defiled this holy place." (What had happened was that they had seen Paul and Trophimus, the Ephesian Greek, walking together in the city and had just assumed that he had also taken him to the Temple and shown him around.)

Soon the whole city was in an uproar, people running from everywhere to the Temple to get in on the action. They grabbed Paul, dragged him outside, and locked the Temple gates so he couldn't get back in and gain sanctuary. (Acts 21:27–30 THE MESSAGE)

When Roman soldiers observed this mob and realized Paul was in danger, they came to his aid. This is just one of many occasions when it's apparent that being a Roman citizen was all part of God's sovereign plan for Paul because his heritage got him out of several tight jams and allowed him to continue preaching the gospel:

As they were trying to kill him, word came to the captain of the guard, "A riot! The whole city's boiling over!" He acted swiftly. His soldiers and centurions ran to the scene at once. As soon as the mob saw the captain and his soldiers, they quit beating Paul.

The captain came up and put Paul under arrest. He first ordered him handcuffed, and then asked who he was and what he had done. All he got from the crowd were shouts, one yelling this, another that. It was impossible to tell one word from another in the mob hysteria, so the

captain ordered Paul taken to the military barracks. But
when they got to the Temple steps, the mob became so
violent that the soldiers had to carry Paul. As they carried
him away, the crowd followed, shouting, "Kill him! Kill
him!" (Acts 21:31–36 THE MESSAGE)

But this dramatic Roman-soldiers-to-the-rescue victory is short-lived because Paul gets mired in the Roman
judicial system, which is evidently even harder to get out
of than the coffee-of-the-month club I accidently signed
up for while surfing the Internet on Ambien. It took him
two years of legal wrangling to simply get his case on the
docket because a dirty governor named Felix kept dragging his feet and slowing the process down thinking he
could squeeze a bribe out of Paul if he let him languish in
prison long enough:

A few days later Felix and his wife, Drusilla, who was
Jewish, sent for Paul and listened to him talk about a life
of believing in Jesus Christ. As Paul continued to insist
on right relations with God and his people, about a life
of moral discipline and the coming Judgment, Felix felt
things getting a little too close for comfort and dismissed
him. "That's enough for today. I'll call you back when
it's convenient." At the same time he was secretly hoping
that Paul would offer him a substantial bribe. These conversations were repeated frequently.

After two years of this, Felix was replaced by Porcius

Festus. Still playing up to the Jews and ignoring justice, Felix left Paul in prison. (Acts 24:24–27 THE MESSAGE)

So, he was forced to play more political chess with Festus, who intended to grease the skids with his Jewish constituents who were lobbying to have Paul transferred back to Jerusalem for the trial. In modern context that would be like manipulating a trial to take place in a city where it was guaranteed there'd be a prejudiced jury, within a state where capital punishment was legal. Fortunately, Paul is able to play his I'm-a-Roman-citizen card again and have his case transferred to Rome to be heard by Caesar on appeal:

> Festus, though, wanted to get on the good side of the Jews and so said, "How would you like to go up to Jerusalem, and let me conduct your trial there?"
>
> Paul answered, "I'm standing at this moment before Caesar's bar of justice, where I have a perfect right to stand. And I'm going to keep standing here. I've done nothing wrong to the Jews, and you know it as well as I do. If I've committed a crime and deserve death, name the day. I can face it. But if there's nothing to their accusations—and you know there isn't—nobody can force me to go along with their nonsense. We've fooled around here long enough. I appeal to Caesar." (Acts 25:9–11 THE MESSAGE)

But then the ship he's loaded on under guard for his transfer to Rome runs into foul weather and they end up shipwrecked off the coast of Malta. After all 276 men on board swim or cling to wreckage and float to the beach like Tom Hanks in *Castaway*, natives greet them warmly and prepare a bonfire to fend off hypothermia. Paul helps gather some sticks for their surfside sauna, and just when you think surely this is the end of the apostle's rotten luck and there's nowhere to go but up, a poisonous snake crawls out of the driftwood, sinks its fangs into his hand, and won't let go.

I know this is beginning to sound more like a Hitchcock movie, but it's not fiction. These outlandish events actually occurred:

Once everyone was accounted for and we realized we had all made it, we learned that we were on the island of Malta. The natives went out of their way to be friendly to us. The day was rainy and cold and we were already soaked to the bone, but they built a huge bonfire and gathered us around it.

Paul pitched in and helped. He had gathered up a bundle of sticks, but when he put it on the fire, a venomous snake, roused from its torpor by the heat, struck his hand and held on. Seeing the snake hanging from Paul's hand like that, the natives jumped to the conclusion that he was a murderer getting his just deserts. Paul shook the snake off into the fire, none the worse for wear. They kept expecting him to drop dead, but when it was obvious he wasn't going to, they jumped to the conclusion that he was a god!

The head man in that part of the island was Publius. He took us into his home as his guests, drying us out and putting us up in fine style for the next three days. Publius's father was sick at the time, down with a high fever and dysentery. Paul went to the old man's room, and when he laid hands on him and prayed, the man was healed. Word of the healing got around fast, and soon everyone on the island who was sick came and got healed. (Acts 28:1–9 THE MESSAGE)

So an unfair accusation led to a would-be lynching, which led to a jail term, which led to political haranguing, which led to more jail time, which led to more political haranguing, which led to a shipwreck, which led to a should-have-been-deadly snake bite, which led to another *revival.* Once again, the seemingly unjust twists and turns of Paul's life lead to the salvation of many who recognized the legitimacy of the gospel because of his white-knuckled loyalty to Jesus and the undeniable power of the Holy Spirit within him, despite persecution and perilous circumstances.

During the two years Paul was under house arrest in Rome, he wrote letters to encourage some of the churches he'd planted on previous missionary trips. Those correspondences are collectively referred to as the Prison Epistles in light of the conditions he penned them in, and they include the four New Testament books of Colossians, Philemon, Ephesians, and Philippians.

Paul stayed on fantasy island for another three months and finally arrived in Rome sometime between AD 59–61, where he was held under house arrest for another two years as his legal case inched along glacially. But his missionary zeal for the gospel didn't suffer while he was stuck in what surely became a claustrophobic surrounding. No, instead Paul exercised his visitation rights, and enthusiastically shared about the life, death, and resurrection of Jesus Christ with all his visitors. As a result, *another* revival took place wherein many Roman Jews with similar bios to Paul's became believers! Which is why he was able to exalt sincerely: "That is why I wanted to see you and talk with you. I am bound with this chain because I believe in the hope of Israel" (Acts 28:20 NCV).

In other words, "Whatever hardship I have to endure pales next to the supernatural hope I'm preaching here, y'all—*Jesus* is the Messiah we've been longing for since the beginning of time!" The joy of watching other people's eyes widen and faces light up when they understood the gospel made all the unfair bumps and bruises Paul experienced along the way more than worth it. The difficult labor was worth the miraculous birth.

ARE YOU WILLING TO RISK BEARING PERSECUTION WITH JOY FOR JESUS' SAKE?

When I was in middle school, my mom gave me her two favorite books to read and told me she believed they contained information that was much more valuable than anything I was learning in school. The first was titled *Through the Gates of Splendor,* and the second was a follow-up titled *Shadow of the Almighty: The Life and Testament of Jim Elliot.*

Phillip James "Jim" Elliot (1927–1956) was born in Portland, Oregon. He was one of four children born to a Plymouth Brethren evangelist and his wife, a chiropractor. An outspoken Christian from his grade-school days onward, he enrolled at Wheaton College in Illinois in 1945, where he fell in love with Elizabeth Howard, the daughter of missionaries to Belgium.

Soon after graduation, Jim began working with the Quichua Indians in Ecuador as a missionary through Wycliffe Bible Translators. A few years after that, in 1953, he and Elizabeth got married. In her classic book *Passion and Purity*, she explains that because of their shared devotion to God and determination not to let romance get in the way of their Christian service, they chose not to have their first kiss until their marriage ceremony. I must confess when I digested that fact, I told Mom I didn't want to emulate *everything* about the Elliots because I wanted to know if the possibility of passion existed with somebody before I agreed to marry him. Of course, now that I'm over fifty and still single, knowing that Elizabeth got married two more times (she was widowed again after Jim) and that those Duggar girls are getting married in their early twenties with only a few chaperoned side-hugs, maybe there is something to the whole no-hanky-panky-until-he-puts-a-ring-on-it perspective.

Anyway, after what was probably a very passionate honeymoon what with all the kissing they needed to catch up on, Jim and Elizabeth continued working as missionaries in Ecuador. Two years later, after a pilot friend named Nate Saint from Missionary Aviation Fellowship told them he'd spotted an unreached people group (the Huaoroni "Auca" Indians) in a dense jungle area as he was flying over, Jim and four other men decided to expand their efforts and establish contact with this fiercely reclusive tribe who'd never heard about Jesus before.

It took them three months of flying over the Aucas and dropping gifts, then setting up camp near their remote village, to generate enough curiosity and trust that three members of the tribe—two women and a man—felt compelled to step out of hiding and meet the missionaries face-to-face. However, after few friendly visits at their campsite, something went horribly wrong. On January 8,

1956, all five missionaries—Jim Elliot, Nate Saint, Pete Fleming, Ed McCully, and Roger Youderian—were speared to death by Auca Indians.

News of their murder caused a sensation in the United States and received major broadcast and newspaper coverage, as well as a cover story and photo spread about the missionaries and their widows and children in *Life* magazine. But instead of responding to entreaties for her and her then-infant daughter to return to "safe" civilization in the United States, Elizabeth chose to remain in Ecuador where, along with Rachel Saint (Nate's sister), they eventually established enough rapport with the Aucas to live in the jungle peaceably among them. Ultimately, Elizabeth was able to see her husband's missional dream realized as many from the Huaoroni tribe put their hope and faith in the unconditional love of Jesus Christ, including several of the men who had actually hurled the spears.[4]

Some have questioned why Jim Elliot and his four murdered friends chose not to defend themselves with the guns they'd brought along to camp for hunting purposes when the Aucas attacked. Or how his wife and Nate's sister could extend forgiveness and grace to the very same men who'd murdered their loved ones. The answer to those questions jumps off the page of one of Jim's journals: "He is no fool who gives what he cannot keep to gain that which he cannot lose."[5]

The term *hope of Israel* was used by Paul a number of times in the last part of Acts (cf. 23:6; 24:15; 26:6-7; 28:20). In his context, it meant that the fulfillment of the Old Testament promises to Israel regarding a Messiah had been realized in Jesus Christ.[6]

That right there is how you and I can endure unfair persecution with more joy like our ancestors in Acts. We have to remember it's for Jesus' sake. The momentary troubles we endure as modern day Christians lead to a divine reward we're guaranteed not to lose because treasures in heaven are impervious to destruction (Matthew 6:20).

WHEN PUSH COMES TO SHOVE AND RISK BECOMES REALITY

It would be the most extreme of exaggerations to boast that I've born a chain for the cause of Christ, because I haven't endured any major persecutions for my faith yet. I mean, one time a university sociology professor accused me in front of the class of having a narrow and naïve mind to believe that Jesus Christ could redeem mankind, but his comments didn't seem all that scathing in light of the accusations Dad Angel had already made in that same vein. Then I had my car keyed by a group of protesters who vehemently disagreed with the views of the ministry I worked for at the time, but it was a white car so it was easy to pretend that jagged silver streak was a pinstripe. Of course, I've already mentioned the confrontation with the robe-clad guy in the rundown apartment complex, and there were a few more doors slammed in my face there after I clumsily attempted to witness. I've been called a few unflattering names when I've shared my faith with unbelievers—"big B-S'er" being the least offensive of those. I was hassled by a few guys I used to race mountain bikes with, but dudes who wear spandex shorts don't have much of an intimidation factor. And of course, there are those snarky online assessments branding me an unfit missionary.

When Paul began preaching in Rome—albeit under house arrest—he was fulfilling the prophetic commission God gave him in a dream: "The next night the Lord came and stood by Paul. He said, 'Be brave! You have told people in Jerusalem about me. You must do the same in Rome'" (Acts 23:11 NCV).

However, I've never been beaten. Or arrested. Or shipwrecked or snake-bit for the sake of the God I love. Compared to Paul, my life's been a cakewalk. Except maybe for the season I shared life with a precious prostitute and hardcore crack addict who'd chosen me to be the adoptive mama of her unborn child. Things did get a little dicey there.

Like the time I was staying with her at the crack house (she didn't get high as often when I was around, so I spent as much time as possible with her for her sake and the baby's) and one of her "johns" knocked on the door. Before she could react, I jumped up from the couch and swung the door open, much to his surprise since he was expecting her. Instead of answering him when he asked if she was home, I looked him directly in his eyes and calmly asked a question that threw him even more off guard, "Are you married?" Now I already knew the answer. She'd confessed that he was one of her favorite customers because sometimes he sprang for a cheap hotel room for their "dates" and then let her spend the night there. She'd watch cable and drink all the Dr. Pepper she wanted while he went home to his wife and five children.

But he didn't know I knew about all that, so he just stood there and stammered. After a few very uncomfortable seconds, I said, "Sir, I know your story. I know you're married and have five kids waiting for you at home. I don't know what else is going on in your life, but you should be ashamed of yourself for coming here and paying for sex with a young woman who has a broken mind and who's seven months pregnant." He mumbled an apology, then turned on his heels, hustled back to his van, and sped off into the night as I stood watching from the doorway with my arms crossed, all bowed up with righteous indignation like some kind of Clint Eastwood character.

The few people I shared the experience with afterwards, including a police investigator, cautioned me not to confront any more drug buyers or johns because it was too risky. They warned me that I was putting myself in harm's way by spending time with her and advised me to just write checks to help pay for her food and care but not be so physically present during the latter months of her pregnancy. I took as much of their advice to heart as I could. I stopped visiting her late at night, when it was most dangerous, but I didn't stop going over there and I didn't stop meeting would-be-perverted-paramours at the door and sending them back to their vehicles with their proverbial tails tucked between their legs.

I just couldn't get past one of her early observations that I was one of the only people who'd ever treated her like she was worth the trouble. It was devastating when I didn't get to be her baby's adoptive mom after all, but she *was* worth the trouble. Every single person on this planet is *worth the trouble* we might face in the context of sharing Christ with them. Plus, every time I remember those johns running back to their cars surely thinking something along the lines of, *That loud, new girl is way too bossy to be a good prostitute!*, I feel an emotion I'm pretty sure is related to pure joy.

Had the best weekend running hard toward Jesus in Houston, first w/a bunch of passionate teenagers then w/a beautiful bunch of friends at Champion Forrest Baptist! God was so gracious ~ we got to watch 7 women launch themselves into the arms of Jesus for the very first time & many more freed from emotional bondage by the Holy Spirit. The fact that Missy was with me the whole time was incredible. I want my daughter to KNOW the amazing grace that sets captives free. I want her to BELIEVE that her Creator-Redeemer is not a faraway dictator but an up-close, personal, perfectly loving Savior she can sprint, stumble or limp toward. And I want her to feel a wonderful sense of security & belonging around older "sisters" who're running the race ahead of her. #clumsysweetcommunion #takeyourdaughtertoworkweekend

(Instagram post from January 2015)

TEN

Kicking Safe, Comfortable

Christianity to the Curb

As shocking as it may seem, I almost refused an opportunity to eat copious amounts of fresh baklava in Greece a few months ago. I've wanted to go there for as long as I can remember, but when Chris and Nick Caine invited me to join them in Thessaloniki—the exact place where Paul and his crazy Christian friends were accused of "turning the city upside down" in Acts 17—I was hesitant. Because the trip would mean being away from Missy for at least four nights, and I wasn't sure I could be away for that long from the daughter I'd only had for six months. Although I've hired an incredible young couple to keep Missy once or twice a month when I'm traveling, I couldn't imagine being away from her for more than one or two nights. I thought my heart might self-destruct with mama-angst if I attempted a four-night separation.

However, after Chris (who's a dear friend and whom I

love more than guacamole, which is saying *a lot*) explained that sometimes brief respites from our children so as to nurture our own souls can be really beneficial for parents, I warmed up to the idea. Then she told me that a few of my modern day heroines of the faith would be on the trip, like Beth Moore, who is my absolute favorite Bible teacher of all time; Lysa Terquerst, who's also a dear friend and just so happens to be a *New York Times* bestselling author yet still finds time to answer my calls and have long talks about mothering and eschatology; and Havilah Cunnington, a young Bible teacher from California who's already accessed the power of the Holy Spirit in ways I'm still dreaming about. So, I decided going to Greece was an opportunity I just couldn't pass up!

Now let me tell you, getting to spend a few days in Greece with Chris, Beth, Lysa, and Havilah was *amazing*. We worshipped until we were hoarse, prayed with astonishing unity and passion, laughed until our stomachs cramped, and enjoyed massive amounts of baked feta together! I love those four girls more than ever before and would gladly give any of them a kidney if they needed it. But, interestingly enough, it wasn't one of those four inspirational powerhouses who impacted me the most on that European mission trip. Nope, it was a young woman whose name I'm not at liberty to divulge because I met her in an A21 safe house, in a rural, undisclosed area that Chris, Nick, and their team have established to care for girls who've been rescued from human trafficking.[1]

For the sake of the story, I'll just call her Priscilla, who was another estrogen-infused gospel heroine. She is first mentioned in the book of Acts along with her husband, Aquila (Acts 18), and her contributions to early Christianity become clear later on in Paul's epistles (Romans 16, 1 Corinthians 16, and 2 Timothy 4). The "Priscilla" I'm talking about now is the first person I saw when we walked into the safe house, and she didn't look at all like the type of girl I was prepared to see. I was expecting to come face-to-face with young women who bore both physical and psychological scars. I assumed they would probably be missing a few teeth due to beatings at the hand of their captors, and their eyes would dart around the room with the kind of alert wariness that comes with being treated like prey for years.

Because of the extensive volunteer work I've done with recovering drug addicts, many of whom worked as prostitutes to support their habit, I had a pretty clear mental picture of the precious, marked girls we'd be meeting in Greece. Language, skin tone, and customs may vary from country to country, but I've discovered that the aftermath of abuse looks pretty much the same whether in Nashville or Nairobi. Surprisingly, Priscilla didn't look anything like most recovering addicts or former prostitutes I've met previously. Instead, she looked like an innocent, happy-go-lucky seventeen-year-old.

She approached me with an ear-to-ear grin and bright, shining eyes that danced directly into mine. Within moments we were making each other laugh with hand gestures and exaggerated facial expressions, because while we didn't speak each other's language, we were both pretty good at charades! I thought, *Oh my goodness, this kid is like a joy bomb just lookin' for a place to detonate*, and felt a momentary twinge of guilt that I was obviously bonding with one of the A21 college interns, because there's no way a young woman as sweet and happy as her could've endured the horrors of human trafficking.

Priscilla and I spent several hours enjoying each other's company, and when the driver told me it was time to leave and return to Thessaloniki, we hugged goodbye for a long time. Then she shyly confided through an interpreter that she wanted to be like me when she grows up and that she wants to travel around the world and tell people about Jesus after coming to America and going to seminary. I felt tears spring to my eyes over the fact that this darling kid, who was already more effective as a missionary than I am, wanted to follow in my bumbling footsteps. I hugged her hard a second time and told her the joy she radiated was already pointing people to the unconditional love of Christ. Then I gave her my e-mail and told her I'd be delighted to connect her to some great seminaries when she got to that point in her journey.

It was only after we drove away from the safe house that I found out Priscilla's backstory. That I found out she was *not* a college intern. How she'd been kidnapped at the age of nine by an organized crime syndicate and smuggled to Greece, where for the first few weeks after her arrival, she was chained to a bed in a filthy apartment and brutally raped multiple times a day by men wearing police uniforms. After raping her, they would leave the room, change into civilian clothes, then come back in with a little food, a little water, and a handful of very addictive narcotics, and soothingly tell her to drink the water, eat a little bread, and take the "medicine" because it would make her feel better and forget what those "mean" policemen did to her. This systematic physical and psychological brutality went on day after day until Priscilla's body was so broken and her mind was so confused that she bent to the will of wicked traffickers who prefer to sell young girls in the sex trade because men will pay a higher price for them.

Priscilla was then put to work in what's called a carousel house in Greece. Prostitution is legal there but with the stipulation that only one girl is on call at a time. Of course, they're supposed to be over the age of eighteen, so traffickers procure fake IDs for babies like Priscilla while people who know better look the other way. To work around the one-girl stipulation and maximize their profits, the organized crime syndicates who run the human sex slave industry there subdivide buildings into tiny, individual bedroom cubicles where porn plays 24–7 and men "get ready." Then one girl, often under the legal age of eighteen, services up to thirty men a day.

Priscilla worked in a carousel house from the age of nine until the age of fifteen when she was rescued in a police raid and sent to the A21 safe house. That is where she heard about the unconditional, redemptive love of Jesus Christ and, against the darkest of odds, believed the gospel to be true. Somehow, someway, through the supernatural power of the Holy Spirit, that precious little girl was transformed from a seemingly irreparably damaged human trafficking victim into a beaming Christ-follower, brimming with hope.

The gospel is *true*, y'all!

The grace and mercy of Jesus Christ have the power to heal and restore that which appears to be broken beyond repair. He really can raise what was dead back to vibrant life. Looking that kind of redemptive miracle in the face sparked a personal revival in my own heart.

Priscilla's miraculous metamorphosis helped me see Jesus bigger and commit to become bolder for His sake.

A SCENIC POINT ON THE ACTS JOURNEY

The last phrase we read in Acts describes Paul as a man who'd seen enough of the redemptive power of the gospel to become a man of big faith and bold actions: "He lived there two whole years at his own expense, and welcomed all who came to him, proclaiming the kingdom of God and teaching about the Lord Jesus Christ with all boldness and without hindrance" (Acts 28:30–31 ESV).

At this point in Paul's story he's confined to house arrest—his second incarceration—and is waiting to go on trial for preaching the gospel. Yet instead of growing bitter or working frantically on an appeal, he's gladly footing the bill for his own orange jumpsuit, all the while welcoming visitors and continuing to witness to anyone who'll listen about the love of Jesus. In spite of the really cruddy circumstances he found himself in, he was radiating the living hope of the gospel without hindrance. These two English words are translated from the single Greek word *akōlytōs,*[2] which is a derivative of the Greek word *kōlyō* Peter used in Acts 11, when he asked the question, "Who was I to stand in God's way?" (Acts 11:17 NLT)

Who am I to stand in God's way? It's a powerful rhetorical question, isn't it?

It's one the Holy Spirit basically knocked me over with a few weeks ago while I was visiting a church in downtown Nashville. About a month after that amazing trip to Greece, my dear, passionate Australian friend Christine Caine came here to Tennessee, to my wonderful, slow-talking, grits-eating, corner of the world, to preach at a church called The Belonging (whose co-pastors, Henry and Alex Seeley, happen to be crazy Australian Christ-followers too). Since The Belonging meets on Tuesday nights, I didn't have to skip services at my home church to attend, so I told Chris I'd be there with bells on in the front row to support her.

And once again, a woman I didn't expect ended up being the powerhouse God used to pierce my heart. Before Chris ever took the stage, Alex introduced a young mom about half my age who grabbed the microphone with gusto. She then gestured to her gorgeous, three-year-old little girl who was wiggling happily in the arms of her daddy and announced, "My daughter was born with a rare blood disease and several specialists told us she probably wouldn't survive infancy." She went on to explain how in the very beginning, she and her husband were devastated, and she wondered why God would allow her baby to die. But then, after spending time on her face before the Lord sobbing, complaining, grieving, and eventually just resting in His presence, the Holy Spirit reminded her that as a believer she had access to the very same power that resurrected Jesus from the grave (Philippians 3:10; Romans 6:4; 8:11).

That's when she decided she had nothing to lose, so she determined to put more faith in the power of the Holy Spirit than she had in the dire prognosis of a team of well-meaning pediatric oncologists. She described how she and her husband began running harder than ever after Jesus, seeking the healing He purchased for us with His stripes (Isaiah 53:5) and praying fervently for their daughter to experience actual physical wellness. They asked their friends to pray and fast too. Their pastors visited them in the hospital and anointed the tiny patient with oil. They all *beseeched* the throne of God's mercy on her baby's behalf.

I'm surprised the roof didn't come right off the building during the crescendo of her testimony when she joyfully proclaimed that the cancer doctors said would kill her little girl was no longer detectable in her bloodstream! Along with most everybody else who attended The Belonging that night, I cheered myself hoarse. But I also cried harder than most because the entire time she was praising God about her daughter's healing, I was holding mine in my lap. And since my little girl has a blood disease as well, I could deeply relate with her.

However, I couldn't help noticing the stark difference between us too. Because while I tend to believe God *can* do anything, that mama believes He *will*.

Mind you, I'm certainly not trying to say that a lack of spiritual faith in the parent is linked to a lack of physical healing in the child. I know incredibly godly moms and dads who've lost children to horrible accidents and diseases. But what I am trying to say is that God whispered that I needed to believe *bigger*. That I had to learn to pray in light of the resurrection power He's promised and hope for some supernatural intervention instead of allowing my hope to be shaped solely by human logic.

WHEN PUSH COMES TO SHOVE AND RISK BECOMES REALITY

Throughout this study of Acts and my real-life experiences that have accompanied it, like becoming a middle-aged single mom to a joyful, strong-willed little girl with HIV and leaving the relative vocational security of speaking on a national Christian arena tour to share the living hope of Jesus Christ in churches and less formal settings around the world, I'm learning to become a much bolder believer.

I'm starting to live with more radical trust, believing God *will* do the impossible, not simply that He *can*. It's been a blast to kick safe, comfortable Christianity to the curb and embrace a wilder walk of faith. Because this Jesus, this gospel really is worth risking everything for.

🔴 Tonight ~ after having the privilege of gabbing about the unconditional love of Jesus to a group of dear women in IL ~ I looked at Missy sleeping peacefully in her hotel bed next to mine & realized I believe in the promises of God more in this moment than I ever have before in my life. He is so incredibly good. "Delight yourself in the Lord, and he will give you the desires of your heart. Commit your way to the Lord, and he will give you the desires of your heart. Commit your way to the Lord; trust in him, and he will act." Psalm 37:4–5

(Instagram post from March 2015)

Speaking of risks, I think it's much more fitting to conclude this book in an unorthodox way, to forgo the format of the previous chapters and give you the space here at the end to commit to a few important risks of your own. Because as my friend Alex Seeley recently observed, "The book of Acts didn't really end in the first century. More chapters of that glorious story are being written through the lives of His disciples even today!" So, I encourage you to carve out a few hours to prayerfully ponder and journal answers to the following ten questions in order to chart a bolder, more passionate future for your own walk of faith.

1. How am I going to live out the risk of actually believing Jesus, as opposed to simply believing "in" Him?

2. How am I going to live out the risk of receiving and welding more power through the Holy Spirit?

3. How am I going to live out the risk of the ongoing act of repentance?

4. How am I going to live out the risk of the give-and-take of real relationships?

5. How am I going to live out the risk of loving more people, more?

6. How am I going to live out the risk of changing my course?

7. How am I going to live out the risk of going somewhere to witness to someone?

8. How am I going to live out the risk of laying aside my preferences for other people's spiritual benefit?

9. How am I going to live out the risk of bearing persecution with joy for Jesus' sake?

10. How am I going to live out the risk of kicking safe, comfortable Christianity to the curb?

Notes

Chapter 1: The Cost of Discipleship

1. C. S. Lewis, *Mere Christianity* (New York: HarperCollins, 2009), 52.
2. Strong's Exhaustive Greek Concordance #2983.
3. Toby McKeehan and Mark Heimermann, "Jesus Freak," Up in the Mix Music, compact disc. Originally released in 1995.

Chapter 2: Earth, Wind, and Celestial Fire

1. Sinclair Ferguson, *The Holy Spirit: Contours of Christian Theology* (Downers Grove, IL: InterVarsity Press, 1996), 12.
2. F. F. Bruce, *The New International Commentary on the New Testament: The Book of Acts* (Grand Rapids, MI: Eerdmans, 1988), 49–50.
3. John Calvin, *Institutes,* III.1.3.
4. Ferguson, 16.

Chapter 3: Checkered Pasts Can Make Incredible Preachers

1. Simon J. Kistemaker, *New Testament Commentary: Acts* (Grand Rapids, MI: Baker, 1990), 87–88.
2. W. E. Vine, *Vine's Complete Expository Dictionary of Old and New Testament Words* (Nashville, TN: Thomas Nelson, 1984), 171.
3. Ibid., 493.

Chapter 4: What's Mine Is Yours

1. www.huffingtonpost.com. Accessed January 18, 2013.
2. Edward W. Goodrick and John R. Kohlenberger III, *Zondervan NIV Exhaustive Concordance* (Grand Rapids, MI: Zondervan, 1999), 1565.
3. Lesslie Newbigin, *The Gospel in a Pluralistic Society* (Grand Rapids, MI: Eerdmans, 1989), 222.
4. www.vancouversun.com/technology/Spanish+runner.
5. Simon J. Kistemaker, *New Testament Commentary: Acts* (Grand Rapids, MI: Baker, 207), 181–82.
6. Jodi Picoult, *Leaving Time* (New York: Ballantine Books, 2014), 356.
7. C. S. Lewis, *The Four Loves* (New York: Houghton Mifflin Harcourt, 1991), 121.

Chapter 5: Loving More People, More

1. Simon J. Kistemaker, *New Testament Commentary: Acts* (Grand Rapids, MI: Baker, 2007), 311.

Chapter 6: Sinners Who Would Be Saints

1. F. F. Bruce, *Paul, Apostle of the Heart Set Free* (Grand Rapids, MI: Eerdmans, 1977), 63.
2. Ibid., 74.
3. Ibid., 16.
4. www.dbts.edu. Accessed June 10, 2012.

Chapter 7: A Compassionate Compulsion

1. www.bu.edu/missiology.

Chapter 8: The Need to Be Regospeled

1. Martin Luther King Jr., Research & Education Institute at Stanford University, http://mlk-kpp01.stanford.edu.
2. Mary Stanton Athens, *From Selma to Sorrow: The Life and*

Death of Viola Liuzzo (Athens, GA: University of Georgia Press, 1998), 5.

Chapter 9: Bearing the Chain Because

1. F. F. Bruce, *The New International Commentary on the New Testament: The Book of Acts*, (Grand Rapids, MI: Eerdmans, 1988), 312.
2. Robert James Utley, *Luke the Historian: The Book of Acts*, vol. 3B, Study Guide Commentary Series (Marshall, TX: Bible Lessons International, 2003), 196.
3. *Homilies on Acts 36.2*.
4. I encourage you to rent the 2005 docudrama, *End of the Spear*, which shares this inspirational story from the perspective of Steve Saint, Nate's son.
5. Jim Elliot, *The Journals of Jim Elliot*, ed. by Elizabeth Elliot (Grand Rapids, MI: Revell, 1978), 174.
6. Stanley D. Toussaint, "Acts," in *The Bible Knowledge Commentary: An Exposition of the Scriptures*, ed. J. F. Walvoord and R. B. Zuck, vol. 2 (Wheaton, IL: Victor Books, 1985), 430.

Chapter 10: Kicking Safe, Comfortable Christianity to the Curb

1. Chris and Nick founded A21 to combat human trafficking around the world. The A stands for "abolish," and their goal is to bring an end to human trafficking in the twenty-first century.
2. Strong's Exhaustive Greek Concordance, 209 and 2967.

About the Author

Lisa Harper is a gifted communicator whose writing and speaking overflow with colorful, pop-culture references that connect the dots between the Bible era and modern life. For six years Lisa was the national women's ministry director at Focus on the Family, followed by six years as the women's ministry director at a large church. She holds a masters of theological studies from Covenant Seminary, is the author of eleven books, several video-based Bible study curriculums, and speaks at churches and conferences around the world.

ARE YOU WILLING TO RISK EVERYTHING?

In this eight-session video-based study, out-of-the box Bible teacher Lisa Harper retraces the steps of the early Christians in Acts and reveals that while they didn't have much of a road map to follow after Jesus ascended to heaven, the Holy Spirit catapulted them forward with so much power, grace, and authority that they dramatically impacted the world. They were willing to risk everything to follow Christ. Are we willing to do the same?